ARTIE'S PARTY

ARTIE'S PARTY

Marylin Westfall Tyrol

ISBN: 9798854731584

For Art and the dedicated board members and many volunteers who support the AWF.

"Friends Helping Friends."

A FEW WORDS FROM THE AUTHOR

First, if you have picked up this book, I want to thank you. Never did I think that I would be a writer, never mind an author of a book. Although I always thought that my brother Art's story would make a good book, I never had the courage to begin or to even think that I could write it. And then…one day I saw a small ad in a local newspaper for a Creative Memoir Writing Course being held in a nearby town. For a couple weeks I couldn't get this course out of my mind. I had never considered writing anything, especially my own memoir. I finally called my longtime friend, Mary, and asked her if she would like to take this class with me. Her first response was, "Oh no, I don't think so, I have nothing to write about." I assured her that she had had a very colorful life and had plenty to write about. So, we made one of those "I'll do it if you do it pacts" and signed up for the class together. This was one of the bravest, most courageous, and best decisions that I have ever made.

The first class assignment was to write a 1,000-word story of our choice or begin our memoir. This is when panic set in… where to start…what to write about? We were asked to submit our paper online for our classmates to read and be ready for them to critique it in class, or we could choose to not submit the paper to our peers beforehand and read it in the class. I wasn't sure I was ready for either and wondered what I had gotten myself into.

Arriving at the first meeting, I found it to be a small class with only eight others and a wonderful instructor, Carole Flanagan Flynn, or "C" as she preferred to be called. "C" laid the groundwork for the class: each writer would have the opportunity to read their paper out loud, there would be no harsh criticism of other's papers, and all comments were to be limited to positive feedback or clarification.

So, this is where *Artie's Party* began. For my class paper, I chose to give Art's story a try. Although I did not submit my paper online for critique beforehand, I did decide, reluctantly, to read my paper that first day in class. I was the last writer to read. When I finished reading and dared to look up…I saw approving smiles and nine pairs of eyes looking at me, holding back tears. That's when I knew that I was meant to do this.

Since that day, I have gone on to write what has become this book. To my surprise and delight, *Artie's Party* has become everything I had hoped for and so much more.

CHAPTER ONE

On a picture-perfect spring day in the middle of May, I noticed the bright yellow forsythia bushes along the property's border and the pink dogwood tree in full bloom in the backyard. Our family had gathered at the big brown dumpster in the parking lot just outside of our mother and stepfather's apartment in a small brick complex in New Haven, Connecticut. This was how we loved to surprise Ma and Gus on special occasions: we would meet at the dumpster, and at the appointed time all converge on them at once. We three Westfall sisters and our families were ready to do it again. This time, Gus, our stepfather of thirty years, was in on the surprise and knew that we were coming to celebrate Mother's Day. Gus was busy making his ever-famous meatballs and braciole with pasta, a huge tossed salad, and warm garlic bread. With all that cooking, I am sure that Ma suspected that someone was going to show up, but she had no idea that all her grandchildren from near and far were in town. Even my son Jeff had taken the train in from Brooklyn, and my daughter Jennifer and her husband had traveled from Richmond, Virginia, with their one-year-old twins to be there for this special celebration. None of us knew that this would be our last Mother's Day with Ma. However, I guess in retrospect, deep down, maybe we all knew.

We rang the doorbell of their apartment, and as soon as Gus opened the door, all eighteen of us piled into their small one-bedroom apartment. Fortunately, the rooms were a good size and the eat-in kitchen opened to the living room, making it one big room.

"Happy Mother's Day, Ma," we all shouted.

Ma and Gus acted like they were surprised and welcomed us with open arms. Ma was delighted to see everyone, but someone was missing: our brother, Art, her youngest and only son. Art was then living at Cape Cod and visited Connecticut only every so often. But when he did, she welcomed him like a prodigal son.

Just as we were settling in, the phone rang.

Gus answered, and after a few words to the caller, he said, "OK, sonny boy; here's your mother. It's for you, sweetie," he said, handing the phone to Ma.

"For me?" she said, batting her eyes like maybe it was a secret lover.

As soon as she heard his voice, Ma's face lit up like a Christmas tree and we all knew that it was Art.

"Get your ass down here sometime, we all miss you," she greeted him in her best West Virginia accent with a bit of motherly guilt.

She held the phone up so we could hear him say, "I know, I know. I wanted to come but I'm flat-out busy," he apologetically said. "We're getting ready for our busy season at Pufferbellies and our summer grand opening is coming up on Memorial Day. Say hello to everyone for me and I promise I'll come down for a visit just as soon as I can. Love you guys."

"OK, but make sure that you keep your promise," Ma said. "We love you too."After that call, we could see that no matter what else happened that day, Ma's day was now complete.

Ma, who was going to be seventy-five in November, was now on oxygen most of the time and was struggling with recurring lung cancer. She had battled the cancer off and on for four years, and this time it seemed to be winning.

"Open your presents, Ma," someone shouted.

We gathered around her, finding seats so we could watch her open gifts. Some shared chairs, some sat on the back of the couch, and some squeezed in on the love seat; others took turns standing. It didn't matter—we were all there, and that's what was important.

Ma liked nothing better than to be at the center of attention of her family. She opened my gift first. I gave her a very beautiful, expensive, soft, blue brushed-cotton nightgown. It was just the kind I knew she would like. It was trimmed with a delicate white lace and small pink satin roses at the neckline and matched her blue eyes. Although Ma had never had much of anything of quality in her life, I knew she would appreciate it. Ma had worked for a short time in the nightwear department of Alexander's Department Store in the Milford Post Mall, and she knew well-made sleepwear.

"Oh, you shouldn't have," she said as she held it up and then hugged it close to her.

I also gave her a special card, one of those that are blank on the inside with space to write your own message. The front had a photograph of a little girl in a black-and-white checkered dress. The single red rose she held was the only thing that had color besides the little girl's rosy cheeks. I remembered struggling to choose a card, since none of the Hallmark Mother's Day cards said what I wanted to say. How do you sum up a lifetime in a card? In my handwritten message, I thanked her for raising us under such difficult circumstances. It had not been an easy life for her, trying to raise four little children in West Virginia in a coal mining town, and it wasn't much easier when our family moved to Connecticut. She had to make ends meet and put food on the table with very little income and an alcoholic husband. The best thing that had ever happened to her was later in her life. After our father passed, she met and married Gus, who adored her.

I also added some humor when I told her that she could be happy that we had not turned out to be like the McMillens. They were a large family on the next street, with six kids who lived in poverty, just like us. They were rough kids with poor hygiene and dirty clothes who fought with each other. They skipped school and often got into some kind of trouble.

"You don't want to turn out like the McMillens," Ma had always warned us.

When she read that out loud, we all laughed and enjoyed the moment, but now as an adult, I wondered what was really going on in the McMillens' house behind closed doors. Did they know what was going on in ours?

After Ma finished opening her gifts, she asked Gus to turn

her recliner around to face the living room so that we could gather around her and some could sit at her feet on the floor. She removed the oxygen tube from her nose, looked around, and smiled at each one of us.

"Come on, Ma, tell us some West Virginia stories," I coaxed her.

Over the years, Charlotte, Eileen, and I, the Westfall sisters, had told our children many stories of our early years of living in a coal mining town in Flemington, West Virginia. But only Ma could make the stories come alive. She had a way of telling the stories with a sense of pride in the lifestyle she had survived.

Ma began by telling us about the backyard gardens being necessary for growing your own food. Each year in the spring, the men of the family hand-tilled the garden plot and the women hoed the rows and planted the seeds. They planted rows of green beans, carrots, peas, beets, potatoes, and even corn.

"Of course we spent all summer watering and weeding the crops," she said, rolling her eyes. "Then," she continued, "we sweated our buns off preparing and canning the vegetables on an old outdoor wood stove. Remember, there were no refrigerators or freezers in those days," she reminisced. "We only had a cold dirt storage cellar under the house and an old ice box in the kitchen. But I must admit," she said, "those canned vegetables tasted mighty good in the middle of winter."

"You know that we had no indoor plumbing, no electricity, no running water, and only a stone well in the yard for water. It had a drop-down bucket with a crank, just like Jack and Jill."

The younger children got a real kick out of that.

"What did you do for a bathroom?" one of the grandsons asked.

"Well, we had outdoor privies—you know, outhouses, small wooden buildings out past the garden. Oh, was that a cold walk in the winter," she said as she rolled her eyes again. "But we did have chamber pots under the beds to get us through the night."

Oh, could she tell stories.

"Tell them the one about the adults going out for Halloween and how after dark they would sneak up and throw raw corn at each other's windows. Or tell them about the custom of the groom pushing the bride in a wheelbarrow down to the railroad tracks and back," chimed in Charlotte, who being the oldest child had more memories of West Virginia than the rest of us.

"No, no, tell the one about living in a chicken coop. We did live in a chicken coop for a while, didn't we?" I asked.

Everyone laughed in disbelief as she assured us that they had fixed up the coop and that there were no chickens in there when we lived in it.

"Whew, good to know," I said, smiling.

Before we knew it, the day was coming to an end, and it was time to say our goodbyes. As we took turns hugging each other and reluctantly preparing to part ways, we all agreed that the day had been too short and that we needed to do it more often.

What we didn't know was that we would be together again in a little more than a week.

Four days later, I got the call that Ma was being taken to

Branford Hospice. Her breathing had become labored and there was nothing else that could be done for her cancer. Her doctor felt she would be more comfortable with twenty-four-hour care.

When I arrived at the hospice that weekend, Ma was already in a morphine-induced coma. I had no idea that I would never have another conversation with her again.

Things moved quickly as we took turns keeping vigil at her bedside, and with the help of the hospice staff, we planned for the end of her life.

Little did I know that I would be giving the nurses in the hospice permission to cut that beautiful blue nightgown off of her less than a week after I had given it to her. I remember thinking, *Oh no, I just spent a lot of money on that nightgown, she loved it, they can't cut it!* Yet I quickly came to my senses and gave them consent when they assured me that it would make things easier for her rather than try to get it over her head.

Art did come that weekend. He had such guilt and remorse for not getting there sooner. As he stood at her bedside, he broke down, and through tears I heard him say to himself, "Always a day late and a dollar short." We assured him that we had no idea that she would take such a quick turn for the worse. He held her hand and talked to her as she struggled to open her eyes.

He said, "Ma, I'm here. I love you." Ma actually smiled, squeezed his hand, and we knew that she knew he was there.

Only a few days later, on another sun-filled day, Art and I hugged each other at Ma's graveside. He always gave the best teddy bear hugs, and I could smell his Old Spice aftershave. Funny—at that moment, I thought of our father, who had always worn Old Spice too.

"Do you think they will be together now?" I asked Art, unspokenly referring to our parents.

"No way," he replied. "She's not going where he went."

I could feel the hurt and anger that Art still harbored about our father, who had passed many years ago when Art was only thirteen. So I dropped that conversation. "Well there's enough blue in the sky to make a Dutchman's pants," I whispered in Art's ear.

This was one of Ma's famous "West by God Virginia" sayings. We really never knew what it meant, but whenever we happen to be together on a blue-sky day, one of us will look up and say, "There's enough blue in the sky to make a Dutchman's pants." This is our affectionate salute to Ma and always will be.

CHAPTER TWO

Art rode to and from Ma's funeral with me in my little blue stick-shift Honda. On our way back to Ma and Gus's apartment, we had little to say and mostly rode in silence.

Art finally broke the stillness by asking, "So how long have you had this car? I didn't know you could drive a standard."

"It's new to me; I have only had it a couple months," I said. "I didn't know that I could drive a stick either." I grinned when I said, "It took a lot of practice with many bucks and stalls, but now I love it."

We were almost to Ma and Gus's apartment when Art quietly said, "Jeez, I have a bit of an upset stomach. Been having some abdominal pain lately."

It was not like Art to complain about anything, so I asked him, "Have you thought of seeing a doctor to check it out?"

"Nah," he said. "It's probably nothing. I'll just ride it out. Maybe it's just old age."

We both laughed as we got out of the car and headed inside to join the others.

The apartment felt strangely empty without Ma. Even though it was a small apartment, it somehow seemed able to hold all of us and our grief too. Reality quickly set in. Ma was gone. What would happen to us as a family? Ma was truly the family matriarch and our own air traffic controller. If any of us wanted to know what was going on in the family, we only had to ask Ma. Everything went through her.

Although Ma and Gus had been married for thirty years, they had married later in life when the four of us Westfall kids were mostly grown. Charlotte and I were married by then and only Eileen, then nineteen, and Art, then eighteen, still lived at home. Gus had never been married before and was thrilled to share Ma's children and eventually her grandchildren. Grandpa Gus was the only grandfather on Ma's side of the family that any of our children knew.

As the grandchildren got involved in activities, Grandpa Gus was right there, ready and willing to jump into their active lives. He could be found at their every sporting event, dance recital, play, or scouting fundraiser. Whether he was running along the sidelines of a football game, cooking hot dogs at a scouting event, or clapping a little too loudly at a school play, he took on the role of proud grandfather.

That day, caught up in the loss of Ma, Gus openly wept as he confessed to us, "You know, now that your mother is gone, my greatest fear is that I will lose all of you too. Her family was my family."

We assured him that we were going to be there for him. We

didn't realize that without Ma, things would be different.

"Let's get Pepe's Pizza! Uncle Art loves Pepe's Pizza," suggested one of the grandchildren. We all agreed, and Gus ordered takeout pizza. As we settled in to wait for it to be delivered, one of the nephews asked, "Uncle Art, tell us some of the stories about when you were growing up?"

"OK, what do you want to hear?" Art sheepishly replied. "The one about the giant clock on the front of our house, or the one about the dog that shit money?"

We all laughed just thinking of these stories. The nieces and nephews, who had heard the stories many times from us sisters, were now grown up in their twenties and could really appreciate Art's storytelling. They laughed hysterically as he told story after story, which only egged him on. Art could truly tell a story funnier than anyone I knew.

"I remember," he said, "the house on East Broadway with the oversized clock with a faded red frame right above the front door. Remember? That's when we lived on the edge of the amusement park at Walnut Beach, right across the street from the Beach Head Bar and Panucci's hot dog stand. Really," he said, "who wanted to be the kids that lived in a house with a big red clock on it? Sometimes on our way home from school, we would walk right past it, like we didn't live there, cut through a neighboring yard, and come in the back door."

Charlotte said, "Art, how about when you were in your twenties and first left home? Didn't you live in a rented room over a strip joint and used to eat donuts from Dunkin Donuts dumpster?"

"Yeah, that's true," Art admitted, shaking his head. Rolling his eyes, he went on to say, "When I lived there, I was only nineteen. My high school buddies would come visit and we would put on a tie, dress shirt, and our best sports coats, trying to make ourselves look older so that we could sneak into the strip show downstairs. Ahh, those were the days," he said, grinning and raising an eyebrow. Art told story after story until the pizza came.

The day came to an end all too soon. Although no one wanted to leave, everyone needed to be on their way home.

As Art made his round of goodbye hugs, he begged us all to come to Cape Cod to see his new apartment. He had just moved into his own place and seemed happy, even though he had recently separated from his wife, Heather.

"You'll love it," he coaxed. "It's right on a water inlet near Hyannis Harbor with a view of Lewis Bay. I have plenty of room."

We all vowed to keep in touch and hopefully visit Art at the Cape. None of us wanted to lose the closeness we felt.

As I drove home alone, I kept thinking about Art and I wondered about all the years we had missed. He had lived on Cape Cod for fifteen years and rarely came to Connecticut. He loved the Cape and considered himself on a permanent vacation. I tried to remember what Art's life had been like after high school and how he ended up at the Cape. I knew that he did not go to college. None of us had. College was not an option. Our family did not have the knowledge or the finances to even consider it. Charlotte, Eileen, and I all worked as secretaries right after high school. Even though Art was a good athlete, he probably was not a good enough student and athlete to attract a college, especially in those days without any help or parental guidance.

Art could always find a job with one of his friends, earning enough to get by. So to the best of my knowledge, he tried a few different jobs, including working at a funeral parlor parking cars, delivering flowers, and serving as a pallbearer when needed. I also got him a job as a maintenance man in a small factory where I worked, but that was not for him. He eventually was hired and trained to work at a finance and credit company. The manager loved Art and saw his potential. This job was a good fit for a while.

In the meantime, when Art was in his early twenties, he married Marcia, his high school sweetheart. Together they purchased a lovely older home in Hamden, Connecticut, which they shared with their dog, Murray, who Art taught to smile on command, and their black cat, Liza. Art and Marcia did not have children of their own but loved our children, their nieces and nephews. They often took a couple of the kids for a weekend and enjoyed spoiling them by eating out and going to a movie or museum. The kids all looked forward to their turn to spend time with Uncle Art and Aunt Marcia.

Art and Marcia were married for about a dozen years, and to our family, it appeared that they enjoyed their life together. They had even taken up skiing in Vermont with a group of their high school friends. Although we knew that Marcia really didn't like the cold or the after-ski drinking and partying scene, it seemed to be a perfect fit for Art.

At some point, Art and Marcia grew apart and amicably decided to get divorced and go their separate ways. We were so sorry to see them break up. Our family loved Marcia, and we knew that our relationship with her would never be the same.

Divorcing and having fewer ties to Connecticut made it somewhat easier for Art to make his move to the Cape.

Art, then in his thirties, took off his dress shirt and tie, left his job in financing in Connecticut, and moved to Cape Cod. He put on a Hawaiian shirt, Bermuda shorts, and flip-flops and never looked back.

So for a few years, Art went to work selling time-shares, tending bar, and soaking up the sun at the Cape in the summers. Then each year, he joined friends skiing in Vermont in the winters where they all worked tending bar or waiting tables at a place called North Country Fair. For Art, this was the best of both worlds. He had found his niche and loved it.

During those years, we sisters, Charlotte, Eileen, and myself, were busy having children and raising our families. We sort of lost contact with Art, as he only came to Connecticut every so often for a holiday or special occasion. Art almost always had a woman or women in his life and seemed to be content dating. We met a few of his women here and there, but none of those relationships seemed serious. He did live with someone for a while and she, Vronnie, although not a skier, joined him going back and forth from Mt. Snow winters to Cape Cod summers.

About ten years after Art had moved to the Cape, he called Ma to tell her that he had met a special woman and that he was getting married. He invited us all to come to his and Heather's backyard wedding. He had excitedly shared with Ma that Heather had three boys, ages six, eleven, and thirteen. Art now had his family. We were so happy for him.

Art was in his glory with his new playmates, as he had always been a kid at heart. He knew how to play. He loved to swim, snorkel, surf, and fish. Plus, he had been a great athlete in his youth, playing baseball, football, and basketball.

Although as we know, married life is not all fun and games, especially raising three boys in a stepfamily situation. Art and Heather were hard workers, both employed in the restaurant industry. Though that can be lucrative at the Cape and the money is good in the summer season, employees receive few paid benefits, and keeping income flowing during the offseason is challenging.

Art eventually took a full-time, year-round job managing Mildred's Chowder House in Hyannis. He did that until his friend, John Morgan, hired him to manage his newly popular nightspot, called Pufferbellies, where Art had tended bar off and on for several years. Pufferbellies became Art's home away from home. He was well liked by the staff and the patrons. He knew how to manage and was great at what he did. He hired, trained, scheduled, and kept the liquor and beverages well stocked. Art treated Pufferbellies as though it was his own business. When Art needed some extra cash, he could always take a shift tending the bar and pick up some good tips for the night. The job was perfect for him, as he loved people and had always loved the fun party atmosphere.

Art eventually helped to convert and open one side of Pufferbellies for country-western dancing. That side of Pufferbellies did not make a lot of money, because country-western dancers are not big drinkers, but the parking lot stayed full, which looked good and helped to bring in steady business for the bar side, especially in the offseason. Art made lots of friends at Pufferbellies and everyone loved him, especially the women. Yes, Art was a handsome ladies' man too, just as our father had been.

I kept my promise to keep in touch with Art. In a phone conversation only a couple of weeks after Ma's funeral, he confided in me that he was still not feeling well. I once again tried to convince him to see a doctor.

"Only if you come visit," he said. "Come on, Marylin; you will love it here. You can walk to the beach from my place, and you can even come dancing at Pufferbellies."

"OK," I said. "I'm coming. I'll be up next weekend."

I could hear in his voice that he was so happy in his new apartment. I'm sure it had not been easy to separate from Heather and her boys after being together for ten years, but he had told me that they had agreed that the best mutual decision was to remain friends and part ways. And remain good friends they did.

On the following Friday, I took the day off from work and drove to Cape Cod. I met Art at his new place. Just as he said, I loved it. It was an adorable apartment over a two-car garage attached to a lovely home in a very nice residential neighborhood. He greeted me at the top of the stairs and gave me a big hug. "Well, what do you think?" he said with the biggest grin on his face.

I stepped into the large, open room and took a look around.

There was a nice-sized beige couch and a love seat, and straight ahead were two single beds tucked into the corners on either side of a sliding glass door. Even though it was one big room, it had a spacious feeling because it was surrounded with tall windows on three sides and boasted a high wood-paneled ceiling. To the right, I could see a small, raised dining area with a table and four chairs leading to a galley kitchen.

"Oh my God, Art; it's awesome," was all I could get out. And I hugged him again.

"I am so happy for you. This is so you and so perfect," I squealed with delight.

"Come on, you gotta see this," he said, grabbing my hand.

He opened the slider to a small balcony. I stepped out and gasped. There it was, just as he had said. We were overlooking a water inlet and a view of Lewis Bay. We hugged again. I closed my eyes, took a deep breath, and the smell of salt water in the air immediately reminded me of living on or near the water in our years growing up along the Milford, Connecticut, shore.

I was so happy for Art and couldn't wait to walk to the beach.

"Let's go," I said. "I can't wait to put my feet in that water!"

We walked arm in arm like two little kids to the end of his street. We found our way down a narrow path bordered with sea grass and fragrant beach roses, which opened onto a small beach. As soon as we reached the sand, without a word, we both immediately took off our shoes and headed for a walk along the beach. On our walk back, Art became quiet. I sensed that something was different.

"What's up?" I asked.

"Well, I just came from my second doctor's appointment," he said.

"And?" I waited as he took a few seconds to gather himself.

"He suspects that I have pancreatic cancer."

Art and I continued to walk along the water's edge, dodging the waves and picking up seashells. Silence filled the air between us, and I didn't know how or where to continue the conversation.

My mind raced with what I knew and what I didn't know about pancreatic cancer. All I could think was, *This is not good.*

Art, being the optimist that he was and sensing my apprehension, said, "Don't worry about it, I've got this."

With the wind at our back and our hair blowing in the sea breeze, we made our way up the path and back to his apartment.

I tried to be present but my mind continued to race. *I don't know anyone who has survived pancreatic cancer. How long will he have? Is this a death sentence? Oh my God, Art is only forty-eight years old!*

Art finally broke the silence and cheerfully said, "I have to work at the club tonight. Why don't you come meet some of my friends? You'll love the music and might even dance."

"OK," I said, attempting to be upbeat. "You're on. I'd love to come."

Art got ready, looking handsome in his pale blue oxford shirt with a Pufferbellies logo embroidered on the pocket, khaki shorts, and leather flip-flops. I didn't know what to wear, so I chose light-colored jeans, a gauzy floral top, and a pair of flats suitable for dancing. "I'm ready, Mr. Westfall, take me to the party," I cajoled.

I knew that Pufferbellies was a popular night club and becoming a Cape Cod legend, but I was surprised to find it located in a historic railroad roundhouse right by the tracks. The parking lot was filled with cars. As soon as we got out of Art's car, I could hear the reggae music blaring from the bar side of the building. The place was hopping. I caught a glimpse of tiki torches lighting a sand volleyball game near the back patio.

Art opened the entrance door. I breathed a sigh of relief when I realized that we had entered on the country-western side of the building. I knew that I wasn't going to be comfortable with the college kids drinking on the bar side. Much to my delight, Garth Brooks's "Boot Scootin' Boogie" filled the room and a good-sized group of middle-aged dancers were whirling around the large wooden dance floor. Art introduced me to a few of his friends and some of the regular dancers. They immediately took me under their wing, inviting me onto the dance floor, and I attempted country-western line dancing. It was not as easy as I had hoped. Just when I thought I had it, the group would make a turn and I would be going one way and the rest of the dancers would be going the other way. I was sure it was because they all had cool boots and I didn't. I vowed to get a pair of cowboy boots just as soon as I got home. I could see Art out of the corner of my eye, smiling like the proud brother that he always was. He was right—I loved it.

I continued to keep an eye on Art all night. I wondered what was going through his mind. I couldn't help thinking, *How do you process a diagnosis like pancreatic cancer?*

I remembered that Art had always been a great dancer. He didn't have a choice since he grew up the youngest of three older sisters who loved to dance. When we were all teenagers, any one of us could be waiting for him to come home from school to practice the jitterbug. He was a great leader, and it sure beat dancing with the refrigerator handle.

In my enthusiasm, I tried to get Art to country two-step with me, but after hesitating for a minute, he said, "No, I'm sorry, but I can't do that. I would like to, but if I dance with you, then I'll have to dance with everyone." I was disappointed but understood that after all, it was his job.

I met many of his friends that night, and several women told me what a gentleman and a great guy that he was, always looking out for them. I wondered how they would handle his diagnosis.

I stayed at Pufferbellies until Art closed the place and we drove home together to his apartment.

"That was so much fun," I said. "And I loved your friends."

"I knew you would," he answered. "Yeah, I'm lucky, they are a good bunch of people."

As we drove the short distance home, my mind wandered again. I just couldn't imagine what Art was thinking about *it*, *it* being the diagnosis he had received earlier that day. Neither of us mentioned it.

The next day Art had to work again, and I decided to go home. We vowed to keep in touch, and I promised to be there for him. That was as close to discussing the problem as we got.

Art walked me out to my car and as he gave me a big hug, I said, "Let me know what they can do. I promise I will come whenever you need me."

"I will," he assured me. "I'll be OK and keep you posted."

I drove away and cried all the way back to Connecticut.

As soon as I got home, I made that hard conference call to my sisters and shared the news with them.

"Now what do we do?" I asked.

The phone went silent. I think we were all in shock, trying to find something to say, some way to fix it, something to hold on to.

Charlotte, the one who does not show any emotion, said, "Well, now that we have him back in our lives, we'll just have to figure it out."

Eileen, who was only thirteen months older than Art and closest to him growing up, was devastated. She quietly said, "All I know is that I am in, whatever it takes."

Without question, we all knew we would be there for Art.

CHAPTER THREE

O ver the next couple of weeks, Art had more tests done. One day he called me and said with encouragement, "My doctor says maybe it's not!" And we were hopeful. But a few days later, he called back and said, "Yes, it does look like it's cancer." He was as disappointed as we were but had held on, hoping for a better prognosis.

Another month went by, and in early August, Art called and said that his doctor wanted to open him up and surgically see what he could do. Art said that he had told the doctor, "Look, I don't have any insurance, but if you keep me alive, you get paid. If I don't make it, we both lose." His doctor seemed to understand, since many of his patients were in the hospitality industry and had little or no health insurance. Cape Cod, being a vacation spot, was home to many food and beverage industry employees—waitstaff, bartenders, dishwashers, cooks, and every level of management. Art was not the only one without health insurance. It was not surprising that the doctor really liked Art, and yet it was surprising that he agreed to do the operation on Art's terms.

The operation was scheduled. We were ready to be there for him, but Art told us not to come as he bravely said, "It's only going to be an exploratory operation and I'll be fine." The Westfall sisters reluctantly agreed not to come.

The operation was scheduled for the same week that I had reserved a little cottage at the Rhode Island shore. I was willing to give up the beach vacation to be with Art, but he insisted, "Have your vacation, you deserve it. I'll be fine."

On the day of the operation, I was at my vacation cottage, attempting to enjoy myself on the beach, but my mind was on Art. Finally, I realized that I could not do it; somebody needed to be there when Art woke up. I needed to be there. A sense of urgency came over me. I got in my car and drove two hours to Cape Cod Hospital in Hyannis.

On my way to the hospital, I passed Pufferbellies, and for some reason, I decided to turn around, go back, and stop at the club. As soon as I walked in, I saw Art's boss and good friend, John Morgan. John had already agreed to call me with Art's results, so he was not expecting me to show up. He told me that he had dropped Art at the hospital early that morning and was waiting to hear from the doctor.

I don't know what came over me, but I couldn't hold back the tears. John comforted me with a caring hug and invited me to sit. We found a quiet corner in the restaurant and sat on opposite sides of an empty wooden table to wait for the doctor's call. I sobbed as I began to tell John some of Art's story. I blubbered what it had been like for us growing up in poverty with an abusive alcoholic father and how Art had been mistreated. I said, "It's not fair…Art had such a tough life and now he has a terminal illness."

John patiently listened to me and asked me to tell him more about our Westfall family. "Well," I said, feeling guilty that I was taking his time, "are you sure you want to hear this?"

"Sure," he said. "We're just going to be hanging out here until we hear from Art's doctor…shoot."

"OK," I said. "Where do I begin…We were a coal miner's family who immigrated from the hills of Flemington, West Virginia, to the shores of Milford, Connecticut, in 1947." I smiled when I said, "At least, to us, it felt like we had come from another country." Flemington was a little rural coal mining town with a population of less than seven hundred. We both laughed when I went on to say, "I recently read that today's population is only about three hundred. It wasn't much of a town, with only a small school, a post office, a one-pump gas station, and a store owned by the coal company. It was a typical coal mining town with railroad tracks running through it to move the coal from the mines. I remember we lived with my grandmother in an old run-down house without indoor plumbing, heating, or electricity."

"So why did your family move to Connecticut?" John inquired.

"Well," I said, "our father was a coal miner, and during World War II, he was drafted into the Marines. While he was in basic training, a grenade accidentally detonated too close to him, bursting his eardrums and causing him permanent hearing loss. He was medically discharged, but he was unable to return to working in the mines, as he could not hear the signals, and there were few other opportunities for employment in the area. Fortunately, my father's Uncle Johnnie lived in Connecticut with his wife and nine children, and he assured my father that if he came to Connecticut, he could get him a job."

"How old were you guys when you left West Virginia?" John asked.

"Let me think," I said. "Charlotte, my oldest sister, was eight, I was six, Eileen was two, and Art was less than a year old."

John still seemed interested and asked, "How did you get to Connecticut?"

I rolled my eyes when I told him, "We rode in a crowded old four-door Ford packed with everything we owned. That old car with running boards and wide tires managed to hold our father, mother, four children, and our Grandma Fern too. The Beverly Hillbillies had nothing on us...except we didn't have a rocking chair on the roof of the car!" I continued, "I remember we ate and slept in the car, only pulling over a few times to get gas or find a grocery store or a bathroom, which was often the woods."

"So...where did you live when you got to Connecticut?" John asked.

"Well," I said, "our family of seven moved into a two-bedroom, third-floor apartment in a three-story seasonal house above our uncle. 'Seasonal' meaning it was drafty, had no insulation, and was not meant for winter living. But we had indoor plumbing, electricity, and heat, albeit only a small portable kerosene heater. And to our surprise and delight, it was located on the Milford shore with the beach as our backyard playground.

Connecticut was definitely a step up for the Westfall family."

"Whew," John said. "How about a drink and a burger, and you can tell me more?"

"Sure," I said. For some reason, just talking about the Westfall family life made me feel a little better. I guess I wanted John to know more about Art's life.

After our break for lunch, John said, "So did your father get a job in Connecticut?"

"Yes," I answered. "But it must have been difficult to find one, as he only had coal mining experience and a sixth-grade education. He did manual labor in a steel factory and eventually became a bartender. Isn't it interesting that Art ended up bartending too?" I mused as though I had never thought about it. "I am sure our father must not have made much money," I rambled on, "as over the years we lived in several seasonal rental houses along the Milford shore. I guess we moved almost yearly, or maybe every time we got behind on the rent. I know we were frequently asked to pay the rent or to leave...always just literally one step ahead of the sheriff. When I thought back about those years and all the moves, I remembered that Ma had a way of assuring us that the next move would be better; we might share a room with a different sibling, we could paint our old furniture another color—maybe we would even be in walking distance to a different school. Or we frequently went back to a school that we had previously attended and were introduced as 'the new kids'...again."

I kept going, reminding John that Art was the only boy and the youngest of the Westfall siblings. The mood shifted when I broke down and cried again as I told John that our father had become an active alcoholic and that I could never understand why he was so mean to Art…especially because he was his only son. I told John of how when our father got angry about something, he would whip his Marine belt off through his pant loops in one quick motion. He would scare the heck out of all of us, but it was always Art who got the worst of it.

Sometimes, when our father wanted to punish Art, he would say to him, "You go out and pick a switch"—meaning a small tree branch—"or I'll pick one for you." John shared with me that Art had told him that our grandmother would sit and hold his hands after our father had used that switch.

To this day, I don't really know what my father's childhood was like growing up in the backwoods of West Virginia, nor can I understand what childhood actions or inactions could have been bad enough for Art to deserve a whipping. It's no wonder that Art had night terrors for most of his life. I don't know why; that day, I wanted John Morgan to know about Art's childhood. I just think I wanted him to know that Art should have had a better life.

Finally, I came up for air and said, "Oh my God, John, I have bored you with our life story. I am so sorry, I don't know what came over me."

He laughed and said, "I loved hearing it. Now let's go to the hospital and check on my buddy."

Come on Marylin, you've got to get yourself together, I told myself as I followed John in my car to the hospital. We parked and went into the hospital together. As we entered the elevator, we were joined by a handsome doctor. I recognized the embroidered name, Dr. Johnson, on his white medical coat. I knew that he was Art's surgeon. I introduced myself and John and asked him how things had gone. Dr. Johnson followed us off the elevator and began to tell us the results. They were not good. He began by saying, "I am so sorry, but I was unable to remove the cancer as it was too far advanced and too close to other organs." He apologized again as he said, "I would not have even opened Art if I had known the situation. But," he continued, "going in had been the only way to find out."

Dr. Johnson paused and said, "I'm sorry there is nothing surgically that can be done, but I will refer Art to an oncologist."

I thanked Dr. Johnson as he gave me a hug, shook John's hand, and left. John and I found a bench in a nearby hallway and sat there, stunned. Neither of us found anything to say.

After a few moments, John said, "Let's go see him."

We gathered ourselves together and went to see Art in the ICU. Art opened his eyes for a minute and acknowledged us with a slight grin but went right back to sleep. We stayed for a while at his bedside until a nurse who was checking on him told us that we might as well leave, as Art would be out of it for quite a while and would need his rest.

John walked me to my car and promised to check on Art every day and keep me updated. I drove back to my vacation spot in Rhode Island, crying all the way.

CHAPTER FOUR

A week went by, and Art was still in the ICU. I called my sisters and we decided that it was time for the Westfall sisters to check on Art in person. Charlotte and Eileen rode together and I drove myself, arriving at Art's apartment at about the same time to drop off our things and refresh before we went to the hospital.

As we went to put our suitcases in Art's closet, we couldn't resist checking out his clothes. Art had always been a great dresser and had the sharpest clothes. At the far end of his closet, we discovered that he had several pastel-colored tuxedo shirts, even a yellow one with ruffles. We also found some fancy brocade vests and a few satin bow ties. Since this was not how Art dressed to work at Pufferbellies, we assumed that he must have worn these for more formal bartending gigs.

Charlotte had a brilliant idea and said, "Why don't we each wear one of his outfits and surprise him?"

The three of us agreed that this would be fun and that Art would love it. There was nothing we Westfall siblings liked better than pulling off the unexpected or shocking each other in a humorous way. We each chose a tux shirt, a colorful vest, and a shiny bow tie. We quickly put them on right over our clothes and off we went. After a short drive to the hospital, we giggled our way up in the elevator and couldn't wait to see Art's reaction. Arriving outside the ICU, we could hardly contain ourselves as we stifled our laughter. We made our way through the double doors into the brightly lit ICU with monitoring machines beeping and staff in scrubs scurrying everywhere. A nurse directed us to Art's bedside in an open room right across from the nurses' station. To our surprise, he smiled like he knew us, but then seemed very disoriented and looked confused. "Oh, you're here," he said. "What are you doing here?"

"We came to check on you and to see if you were behaving yourself," I said with a smile.

The head nurse who was standing nearby must have sensed what was going on. She motioned us aside and reprimanded us for not taking an ICU patient seriously. She sharply drew the curtains on either side of Art's bed and walked away. We looked at each other, realized what we had done, and immediately took off the vests and bow ties.

Art knew us for sure, but he went in and out of slumber and couldn't seem to focus on reality. At one point, he whispered in my ear, "See that one over there?" He pointed to the nurses' station. "She's the head of it all. They are going to have a gathering tonight, and I think they are planning on killing me." I tried to assure him that he was safe and that everything would be OK. Things seemed to go from bad to worse when, at his request, Charlotte handed him what she thought was a blue mouthwash. After he took a good swig, coughed, and made a face, she realized it had been a bottle of aftershave. Art continued to not make any sense as he tried to form sentences. We were scared and didn't know what to do next. I decided to talk with the head nurse.

"Listen," I said to her. "He is not himself, not making any sense, and is hallucinating. We wonder what can be done. Do you think it's the meds he's taking?"

"I really don't know, but I will contact his doctor," the nurse said.

Very shortly, the nurse came back and told us, "His doctor explained that the operation had been ten hours, and often a person being sedated for that long has side effects, including possible paranoia." He also suspected that Art could be sleep-deprived—a condition that happens to patients in extended stays in the ICU. The nurse went on to say, "The doctor has suggested we move him to a regular floor, and there's a room available, so we will move him as quickly as possible."

"Thanks," I said. "That sounds like a good plan."

We stayed with Art until he was settled in his new room and sleeping comfortably. We had only planned a short visit to the Cape; however, one look at each other and without saying a word, we all knew that we could not leave Art. Not yet. With heavy hearts, we retreated back to Art's apartment to stay another night.

The next morning, the three of us went back to the hospital, and to our great relief, Art was sitting up in bed and had just finished his breakfast. The move to a quiet, sun-filled room seemed to have been just what he needed. Although he was a little pale and needed a shave, Art already seemed more himself and was glad to see us. He smiled and said, "Well, look who it is. The Westfall sisters are back in town. You know that you guys didn't have to come?"

"Why not," I said. "We love staying in your apartment, and besides, we wanted to check on you to make sure you were OK."

We pulled up chairs and sat by his bed, visiting with him for an hour or so.

We knew he was feeling better when he said, "I gotta get out of here and get back to work." I caught Eileen's eye and wondered if she was thinking the same thing that I was: *Will he be able to go back to work? Will he be able to go home and be alright on his own?* We were all quiet for a moment and then Eileen asked him, "Art, do you want one of us to stay with you for a while when they let you go home?"

Per usual, Art said, "Nah. Don't worry about me. You guys have your families, and when they let me go home I'll be fine. I have lots of friends here on the Cape, and the doctor promised to send a cute nurse to check on me."

The three of us would have loved to have stayed with Art, but since we each had jobs and responsibilities at home, we agreed that we would head back to Connecticut, even though our hearts were heavy with worry for him. Once again, as we said our goodbyes, Art promised to keep in touch with us, and we agreed to come back to the Cape soon.

A few days later, Art did go home to the apartment that he

loved so much. His friends stopped by often to visit and brought him meals from his favorite nearby restaurants—chowder from Spanky's, a burger from The Black Cat, and even a BLT from The Mooring. Heather, his ex-wife, became one of his regular visitors. She knew what he liked and nourished him with her great home-cooked meals. Over the next couple weeks, Art slowly gained his strength back, and before we knew it, he was right back doing what he loved—managing Pufferbellies.

While Art was in the hospital, he didn't know the word was out about his diagnosis and the troops were circling the wagons on his behalf. His friends and coworkers in the restaurant and entertainment industry knew that Art did not have health insurance, and just like most of them, he only had income when he worked. At that time, very few hospitality workers had sick pay benefits and they derived most of their income from gratuities. I will always remember that no matter how much money Art had in his pocket, he always left a generous tip. Over the years, whenever the three of us girls went out for a meal with Art, either he would insist on paying, or we would fight to share the bill. When we put our share of the check down on the table, along with what we thought was a reasonable tip, Art would say, "Are you done?" Then he would add an extra five, ten, or even twenty dollars to the gratuity. To this day, when the three of us sisters eat out together, we always add an extra tip, saying, "This one's for Art."

It was not long before Art's closest friends organized a fundraiser for him. Before Art even knew about it, Artie's Party was already in motion. At first when he found out about the event,

Art was embarrassed and tried to call them off. But that was not going to happen. He was one of theirs, and they were going to do what they could to help him. Plans for the fundraiser spread quickly around the Cape and even people who did not personally know Art wanted to be a part of it. John Morgan donated the use of Pufferbellies for a Sunday afternoon party. Six local bands offered to play for free, a couple of DJs volunteered to keep the music going, bartenders and waitstaff signed on to donate their time, and several food and beverage vendors generously offered to provide a buffet meal. Artie's Party was happening! The committee put together raffles and giveaways. In addition to the entrance fee of $20, each person was asked to donate a scratch lottery ticket. Art's friend and committee member John Shea even designed a special baseball cap for the event. The white hat was embroidered with "Artie's Party" and had a colorful cocktail glass, complete with a red cherry and a flag stirrer. This party was going to be something special, and Art was to be the beneficiary of it all.

In early September, close to his forty-ninth birthday, Artie's Party happened as planned. It was a fabulous event and well attended by friends and family from near and far. Pufferbellies was packed and hopping as one band after another took their turn on the stage. Art did not seem to be feeling his best, although he tried to cover it up. I noticed that he was pale and looked tired. He sat in a booth with family, and every so often, I caught him wincing with his hand on his abdomen. At times, he had a faraway look and seemed overwhelmed with it all. I wondered if the benefit fundraiser had made his plight feel a little more real.

He was thrilled to see so many people and sheepishly enjoyed the celebration in his honor. I could only imagine his thoughts. *Would he live to enjoy more times like these? Did he deserve such an outpouring? How could he ever pay them all back?*

Artie's Party was a huge success, bringing in thousands of dollars and hundreds of scratch lottery tickets. From the comfort of his lounge chair at home that night, Art grinned and rolled his eyes as he asked, "Whose idea were these tickets anyway?" We all laughed as he continued to scratch and scratch. I can't remember the amount he won from those tickets, but I know it was in the hundreds. A few days later, Art was surprised and grateful to find out that the proceeds from the event had paid for most of his doctor's bills.

CHAPTER FIVE

I n the meantime, Art met with his oncologist, Dr. Brown, and started treatments. While there were no promises for healing and little hope for remission, Art agreed to try chemotherapy. Initially, Art seemed to handle the chemo treatment better than most, escaping the side effects of nausea and hair loss. Even though he was often very tired from the treatments, he pushed through it and went back to work at Pufferbellies after each session. Art managed to continue working and kept his spirits up. The rest of us worried and prayed for him.

As Art seemed to be holding his own, the Westfall sisters went on with our own lives in Connecticut and Art continued to live his life at the Cape. The good news was, Art actually began coming home to Connecticut more often. He visited with his old high school friends in Milford and came home to be with our family for Christmas that year. We were thrilled, as it was the first time in a long time that Art had joined us for a holiday.

For a few months, we all wanted to believe that he was going to get better and beat pancreatic cancer, but that was wishful thinking.

In a phone conversation sometime in early spring, Art reluctantly told me that Dr. Brown, his oncologist, or as Art now affectionately called him, his "poisonologist," advised him that the chemo treatments did not seem to be helping. After receiving this news, Art did what anyone with his diagnosis would do... he bought a convertible! Since the committee had paid for most of his medical bills, why not? Art loved driving that car with the top down every chance he got.

A new convertible was enough of an excuse for the Westfall sisters to make a trip back to the Cape to check on Art. On our last visit to the Cape, Art's landlord, Alice, had said to us, "You know, Art is always so excited when he knows that you're coming. With a twinkle in his eye and a smile on his face he said to me, 'Batten down the hatches, the girls are coming to town.' He loves it!"

When I told Art we were coming, he said, "Look, why don't you girls use my place and I'll stay someplace else." But I knew the Westfall sisters were having none of that and said, "No way, what fun would it be without you joining our PJ parties?"

So in early June, we sisters went back to Hyannis.

Since we each drove from different parts of Connecticut, it was amazing that we arrived within minutes of each other. When I drove up, I saw Art was on his balcony waiting for us. He was grinning from ear to ear and seemed glad to see us. He came right downstairs to help us with our bags.

"Jeez," he said, laughing. "Are you guys coming for the weekend or moving in?"

Eileen had a suitcase and two soft-side bags along with a

thick, fluffy bathrobe over her arm and two bed pillows with satin pillowcases. Charlotte had an armful of clothes on hangers, a big suitcase, and her iron with the cord dragging on the ground. I managed with an overnight bag, a canvas beach bag, and my camera bag. The Westfall sisters were never known for packing lightly.

As soon as we dropped our things on our chosen beds, we all headed to the balcony to enjoy the view. We were welcomed by a warm breeze, the smell of the ocean in the air, and a few boats in the distance. "Not a bad place, huh?" Art said as he proudly looked out, as though it was his estate. As we continued to gaze out over the creek below and to Lewis Bay in the distance, there was an unusual silence among us. I wondered if others were thinking the same thing I was...*How much longer do you think Art has to enjoy this view?*

Art broke the silence when he said, "Well, are you girls up for a ride in my new car?"

"Of course," I said. "That's why we're here!"

It was not quite beach weather, but always warm enough for a ride in a convertible. "Let's go," Charlotte said as she put on her yellow straw hat with a rolled-back brim and big, hot pink flower right in the front. Eileen looked at me as she rolled her eyes toward Charlotte as if to say, "Check this out." In return, I tilted my head and scrunched up my shoulders in disbelief. "What?" Charlotte said. "You don't like my hat?"

"No, no," I said, trying to get the look of astonishment off my face. "Just thinking it might blow off in the convertible with the top down."

"It will be fine," she said. "And if not, I'll just hold on to it and do a Mary Poppins."

We all laughed out loud with a vision of her flying off, holding on to her hat.

Eileen asked Art, "Is it OK if I wear one of your baseball hats?" There were many hanging on pegs all around the room.

"Me too?" I asked.

"Sure, help yourselves," Art replied. "Are you girls ready yet? Let's go."

On the way down the steps, Charlotte yelled, "Dibs on the front seat."

But of course she would sit in the front. Since she was the oldest and thought she was in charge, we affectionately always let her have her way. She is the queen bee.

We came around the corner of the garage and there it was, a metallic bronze Chrysler LeBaron convertible with light tan leather bucket seats. The top was already down. Art and Charlotte slid into the front seats, Eileen and I jumped into the back seat, and off we went. We were like a bunch of teenagers on a joyride. Riding alongside the beaches of Hyannis and Centerville, I felt like nothing could be better than the four of us sharing this beautiful sun-filled day. "Wait," I said. "Pull over here right by those rocks; let's take a picture." It was a great spot on a dead-end street with a sandy beach and the ocean in the background. I so wanted this picture, but how were we going to get one of the four of us? Remember, this was in the "olden days" before selfies. Just then I saw an attractive forty-something woman walking toward us along the water's edge. I jumped out of the car and asked her to take our picture. She readily agreed. Art got out of the car and politely introduced himself, and as though to apologize, told her we were his sisters. "Thanks for doing this," he said. "They're never going to be happy unless we get this picture."

She laughed and said, "Oh, no problem. Happy to do it."

I handed her my camera and showed her how to use it. She took a couple pictures of us in the convertible, then handed my camera back to me. We thanked her and she walked away. I noticed she took an extra look at Art. I nudged him and said, "Hmm, did you catch that? She seemed to have an eye for you." It no sooner fell out of my mouth when I immediately realized what I had said. Art gave me a puzzled look with a raised eyebrow, like: *Yeah, sure…I've got a diagnosis of a terminal illness and you want me to pick up this chick?* I guess I wasn't thinking. I knew he was right, but I just didn't want to believe it. The others did not hear our exchange, so we picked up the pieces and went on with our afternoon. As it turned out, this was one of the last photos with Art and my favorite picture of the four of us.

We continued to ride along the shore, stopping for a late lunch of chowder at a cute little clam shack across from the beach, and eventually made our way back to Art's place. We truly were enjoying our time together, yet there was always that elephant in the room—no one dared to bring up the cancer diagnosis. Did we think if we didn't talk about it, it would go away?

Back at Art's apartment, while we were sitting around just hanging out together, Art finally confessed that he was in a lot of pain from his big toe. That's when I noticed that his toe was black and blue and swollen around the nail. It looked like it would be very uncomfortable to wear a shoe.

Eileen asked, "Art, why don't you let me clean it and put a bandage on it?"

"Nah," he said, brushing it off. "It's not that bad. Maybe later."

I asked, "Did you ask your doctor about it?"

"Yeah," he answered. "My doctor doesn't seem to know. He said possibly gout, or a side effect from the treatments, or maybe a circulation problem. He suggested that I get a special orthopedic shoe to relieve the pressure." Art then scrunched his face as if to say, *I'm not doing that.* "Don't worry, it's really nothing," he said as he tried to cover it up and make light of it. But after he thought about it for a minute, he sheepishly asked me, "Will you come with me to the drugstore? Let's go check out the damn shoes."

"Sure," I said, tipping my head toward Eileen and Charlotte. "Looks like these two are ready for a nap; let's go do it."

Once again, Art drove the back roads to a drugstore, avoiding all the Cape tourist traffic while we enjoyed the gentle warm sea breeze in his convertible.

"How do you like my car?" he said.

"Love it," I said. I looked away and stared off to the side, wondering how long Art would have to enjoy it and what was going to happen to him next.

We easily found the pharmacy in a small strip mall. Getting out of the car, Art said, "Jeez, I don't want to die from a lousy toe, that would be so lame." We both burst out laughing and hugged our way into the drugstore. There wasn't a great selection of open-toed orthopedic shoes, but we found a leather Dr. Scholl's with a double strap that looked like the Birkenstocks that the hippies used to wear. I convinced him that if no one looked down at his feet, they would not realize he sported one flip-flop and one open-toed orthopedic sandal. He reluctantly agreed. "High five," I said as we slapped hands and left the store arm in arm, satisfied with our purchase.

Riding back to his apartment, Art and I cooked up a scheme. It was our sister Charlotte's birthday, and he wanted to surprise her with a cake that night at Pufferbellies. Since Charlotte had always been not only the queen bee but also the queen of "gotcha," here was our chance to get her back. When we were kids, Charlotte had been known to jump out of dark closets or hide behind shower curtains to scare the bejeezus out of us every chance she got. Or she would embarrass us in public any way she could. Art said, "This will be great! I'll get the cake."

"I've got it," I exclaimed, yelling over the song on the radio. "How about having a couple of your bartenders present it to her, maybe even like the Chippendale dancers!"

"OK," he said, laughing. "I can't promise, but I'll try to get a couple guys to do it." When we got back to the apartment, I sneaked Eileen aside and told her of the plan. She and I couldn't contain ourselves, bursting into laughter with the thoughts of "getting Charlotte."

That evening, Art went to work at Pufferbellies and we sisters joined him later. It was a Saturday night, and the place was packed. Art ushered us to a booth near the bar overlooking the dance floor on the country-western side and we settled in. At the appointed time, the DJ started playing something about "this old hat" (which Charlotte often wore). Out of nowhere came three bare-chested bartenders, wearing only bow ties and low-cut jeans and carrying a huge birthday cake. The whole place sang "Happy Birthday." Charlotte was shocked and turned beet red when she realized the cake was for her. She was beyond surprised. The plan had worked and was perfect. We got her this time! The cake was huge and beautifully decorated with pink roses. It was almost like an Italian wedding cake, which must have set Art back at least two hundred dollars, but it was worth it. Oh, how we loved it! Charlotte cut the cake and served it to everybody in the place. It is a memory that we all hold dearly and still laugh about each year on Charlotte's birthday. In the midst of the celebration, I glanced at Art, who was beaming and enjoying the moment. I wondered if he would be around for his birthday in September. We laughed for the rest of the night at the huge success of our surprise. Later that evening, back at Art's apartment, we continued to high-five and congratulate ourselves on pulling off a great one. Waking up the next morning, we started laughing all over again. This remains one of the bittersweet memories of the times we spent with Art at the Cape that special summer.

Since we are not a family known to share our feelings, we managed to get through the weekend without really talking of Art's progressing pancreatic cancer. But when it came time to say our goodbyes, none of us could hold back our tears. Art held on to Charlotte as though he might not ever see her again.

We sisters left in our separate cars, and it was a good thing that each of us had a tissue box on our front seats. Like Charlotte and Eileen, I cried all the way home to Connecticut.

CHAPTER SIX

After telling my daughter Jennifer about our sisters weekend at the Cape and how we had surprised Charlotte with a birthday cake at Pufferbellies, she laughed when she said, "OK, Mom, now Uncle Art really is going to die. He finally got one on Aunt Charlotte."

She then said, "You know what? You guys have had so much fun visiting with Uncle Art, I have an idea. What do you think if I ask my brother and our cousins to go to the Cape to visit Uncle Art?"

"I think it's a great idea. He'll love it!" I replied with enthusiasm.

I paused and thought about it for a minute, and although I did not want to believe it myself, I said, "I know that this is hard to hear, but I would do that visit sooner rather than later."

The very next week, Jennifer rallied her brother Jeff and their cousins, Art's nieces and nephews who were all young adults in their twenties. Knowing that Art's prognosis was not good, they wanted to spend a weekend with Uncle Art too. Jen came from

Virginia and Jeff from NYC, and they joined several of their Connecticut cousins, Scott, Randy, and Kent (Charlotte's sons). They all converged on Uncle Art's apartment. Just like us sisters, they wanted to stay at Art's place with him too. They crashed on his couches, his two single beds, and even brought sleeping bags for the floor. No one cared where they slept; they just wanted to spend time with Uncle Art.

I don't know all that went on that weekend, but I know that one evening they had dinner with Uncle Art at the Harbor and then partied at Pufferbellies while he worked. Of course, Uncle Art covered their tab at the bar, so it was extra fun. From what I heard about the weekend, what they enjoyed most was being together at Uncle Art's apartment. Jeff did share with me that one of the nights when they were just hanging out, someone suggested to Uncle Art, "Why don't you try smoking pot? It might help reduce the pain." Jeff said Art laughed and replied, "Yeah, I tried that once, but after I scraped myself off the ceiling and stopped chasing small animals saying, 'Come here, little buddies,' I decided it wasn't for me. And it actually didn't seem to help the pain."

On the last night of the cousins' visit, they cajoled Art into telling some stories about growing up in Milford. They begged him to tell the one about the big red clock...again.

So he told them about one of the several places that we had lived on East Broadway in Milford, a house on the main street of the Walnut Beach section of town. The beach and Long Island Sound were across the street, only a block away. In the spring and summer, it was almost like living in a carnival. He remembered that there was a merry-go-round, bumper cars, lots of food vendors, and many games. The thing that he remembered most was the huge red wooden clock, two feet in diameter, right on the front of the house above the entrance door. It had fancy gingerbread trim and reminded him of the witch's house in Hansel and Gretel. "Jeez," he had said. "Who wants to live in the witch's house?" He went on to remember that the hands on the clock were stuck at ten of three. At least that's what it always said on his way home from school every day. He got them all laughing when he told how he was so embarrassed to live there because it looked like we were living in a gift shop, a beauty parlor, or maybe a pawn shop.

The cousins had heard many stories of growing up in Milford from their mothers, the Westfall sisters, but it was always more fun to hear Uncle Art tell these stories with his humorous twist. "Alright, here's one more for ya," he said. "I guess I was about eight years old when I finally got my own room after several years of sharing a room with my grandmother." Well, it was sort of a room...it was a very small unheated enclosed porch, which was on the second floor and jutted out over the roofline with windows on three sides." He kept them in stitches as he continued, "Get this: I had an old metal bed on wheels. On stormy nights, the wind rattled the weathered windows and shook my bed. Sometimes it even moved me across the linoleum floor, which was on a slant. Jesus," he said. "I used to pull the covers over my head when there was a thunderstorm, as I was afraid of lightning striking that old iron bed right through those windows." Art kept them laughing until their sides hurt.

Jen told me that at one point, Uncle Art seemed to be day-dreaming and looking off into the distance. He teared up when he told them how he, being the youngest, got dragged along with his sisters wherever they went: the movies, rollerskating, the beach, and whatever else they came up with. But now as he looked back, he was so grateful they had always taken care of him.

From all reports, I believe the cousins had a great weekend. They speak fondly of how they spent one last weekend with Uncle Art. The next time they would be together again at the Cape would be to celebrate Art's life.

CHAPTER SEVEN

Considering that Art's diagnosis of pancreatic cancer had been almost a year ago, he had held his own, surviving longer than most. He underwent several rounds of chemotherapy and yet was still able to maintain his job as general manager of Pufferbellies. Art was one of the lucky ones who did not lose his hair from chemo treatments. Since he was only forty-nine, his thick hair had just started to gray at the temples, enchancing his boyish good looks and adding a distinguished charm. I imagined when he had his treatments, he was the talk of the waiting room, comforting and encouraging others who were also seeking the magic cure and hoping to be cancer survivors.

Art and I kept in touch by weekly phone calls. This week when we spoke, I cheerfully asked, "So, what's going on?"

"Ah, not much. You coming up?" he asked.

"Yeah, sure; I'll be there on Friday," I replied.

After a little more small talk, he said, "Might as well tell you, Dr. Brown called me today and he told me that the chemo treatments are not working like he had hoped and that there really was nothing else he could do."

My heart sank. Art was his optimistic self, and hearing my silence, he said, "Now don't go worrying. I've got this."

It was such a shock to hear. I stumbled through some supporting words and said, "I'll be there this weekend."

The next day, I went to my regular therapy appointment, and as I sat down on her couch, I collapsed in a puddle of tears. I told her of Art's new prognosis.

She asked me, "What do you need? What do you need to do for you?"

I blubbered, "I don't know…What can I do? He lives by himself and he's going to need someone."

She just listened and let me ramble on: "I want to be there for him, but what about my job?" I went on talking. "You know that I am the office administrator and advertising director; I can't just walk away…What can I do?"

She sat quietly as I tried to gather my thoughts.

After a long pause, I said, "I know that the most important thing for me is to be there for him." All of a sudden, after hearing myself say this out loud, I knew what I needed and wanted to do. I decided then and there that using my vacation time on days to visit Art was an option. And so I did. I committed to a weekly journey to the Cape to be by Art's side and walk that walk with him. I began a routine. On Thursday nights, after squeezing in a full week of work in four days, I cooked a meal or two to take with me. I also packed a cooler with some fruit, veggies, cheese, and yogurt. Friday mornings, I drove to Cape Cod, looking forward to spending the weekend with Art.

On a beautiful July day, arriving while Art was at work, I found his spare key right where he left it for me, tucked behind some books on the bookcase in the breezeway. I made two trips, bringing my suitcase and the cooler upstairs to his apartment. I put the food in the refrigerator, wasted no time putting on my bathing suit, threw on a cover-up, and walked to his nearby neighborhood beach to enjoy the afternoon. I flipped off my sandals, placed my beach towel on the warm sand, and settled in. It felt wonderful to just let the sea breeze blow through my hair. I brought a book to read but didn't bother to pick it up, as I was content to daydream and watch the boats and ferries go by in the distance.

At some point, I noticed a man coming toward me, slowly walking along the water's edge. As the man got a little closer, I realized it was Art. Could it really be him? Had I been oblivious over the past month that he was losing weight, or had he suddenly dropped weight in the past two weeks since I had last seen him? I didn't know what to do, but I knew that I had to get that look of shock and astonishment off my face before he got closer. By the time he was almost to where I was sitting on my beach towel, I had sucked the tears back in and put on a reasonably happy face. I stood up and we hugged a little tighter than usual, a knowing hug that seemed to say, *Let's not talk about it or say it out loud and maybe it will all go away.*

"Come on," he said. "I have to get ready to go back to work. You're going to come tonight, right?"

"Sure," I said. "I'm looking forward to it."

It was Friday night, and Art left early for his scheduled shift at Pufferbellies. I happily agreed to join him there a little later. Arriving at Pufferbellies, I looked around and found Art in the crowded balcony. From across the room, I couldn't help noticing how happy he was in his element, smiling and enjoying himself among the summer crowd. I could see most everyone had a drink or a beer, and some were even balancing their drinks in one hand as they danced to the loud DJ music. For a few minutes, I continued to watch Art from a distance. My heart ached knowing what I knew about Art's latest prognosis. He saw me and came right over. "So happy you're here," he said, giving my shoulder a squeeze. Beaming and grinning like a proud father, Art introduced me to some of the regulars. "Hey, this is my sister, Marylin," he said over and over again as we made our way through the crowd.

At one point, he affectionately grabbed me by the arm and gently pulled me across the room as he shouted over the music, "Come on, I want you to meet someone special."

He stopped in front of a couple and said, "This is my poisonologist, Dr. Brown, and his wife, Sarah."

"Oh," I joyfully said, reaching out for the doctor's hand. "I am so happy to meet you."

To my surprise and delight, Art's oncologist and his very pregnant wife had found time to come see where Art worked. I was so touched, especially since only a few days earlier, Dr. Brown had told Art the bad news that he had run out of options for treating him. After our introduction and a short conversation, Art excused himself as he was called away to help at the bar. I stood there with Dr. Brown and his wife, trying to think of something to say. Thankfully, Dr. Brown found a seat for his wife and motioned to me to follow him to a less noisy corner where he said, "You know, it breaks my heart not being able to do anything else in the way of treatment for Art. The cancer is not responding the way that I had hoped it would."

I just nodded my head as though I understood.

"Your brother is a very special guy. Just look at him; he has a smile on his face, and you would never know what he's going through. If I asked anyone in this room tonight to look around and find a man with your brother's terminal diagnosis, they would never choose Art."

"Thanks for all you have done for Art," I said, not knowing what else to say.

As he and his wife gave me a hug and said their goodbyes, Dr. Brown whispered in my ear, "Your brother has given more to me than I could ever give to him. He's a brave and courageous man."

That night, I stayed at Pufferbellies until Art was ready to go home. As we made our way up the steps to his apartment, I decided to try and talk about it. I wanted him to know that I was open for him to be able to talk about what he was feeling and especially what it was like for him to be facing dying. I had been attending college at night, working toward a drug and alcohol abuse counseling degree. I had recently completed an Elisabeth Kübler-Ross course on the stages of death and dying. Getting an A in the course, I now fancied myself somewhat of an expert on the subject. Of course, that was not true.

As was our custom, before going to bed, Art and I went out on his balcony to check the night sky. It was a warm, star-filled night, with a bright moon looking back at us. That night, the view was breathtaking. We both gently leaned on the railing with our hands under our chins like two kids mesmerized by watching fish in an aquarium. Not wanting to interrupt the beauty of the moment, I mused, "Did you ever think about what's beyond the stars or where we go when we leave here?"

"Nah," Art gently said. "I look at it this way: make the most of your time here and don't worry about what happens after that."

After a few minutes, I decided that it was now or never. I took a deep breath and softly said, "Art, you know that I just took a course on death and dying, so if you ever want to talk about it, I'm here to listen."

He didn't answer right away and just kept looking out at the night sky as though he was thinking it over. He finally broke the silence when he said, "Look, I know that you are excited about getting your degree in drug and alcohol counseling, and don't get me wrong, I am excited for you to do that too." He raised one eyebrow, looked at me out of the corner of his eye, and continued. "But are you sure you are up to dealing with drug addicts and alcoholics? They can be a really challenging group, and no offense, I look at you like Bo Peep in the bullpen."

I covered my mouth with my hand and we both burst out laughing.

I replied, "I know that you don't think I am tough enough to handle these types of people, but my heart is in it, and I'm going to give it a try."

He shook his head and hunched his shoulders. "OK, Marylin Kay, if you think you want to do it, I'm all for it," he said with a warm smile.

Well, so much for my expertise on death and dying. Art had successfully changed the subject, and I accepted that he had no interest in talking about *it* or going "there." I never brought it up again. Art put his arm around me and gave my shoulder an affectionate squeeze as we walked back inside. At least I went to bed that night with a smile on my face, knowing that we didn't exactly talk about *it* but that Art knew I was there for him.

Early the next morning, as Art and I were having breakfast on his balcony, the phone rang. Art went inside to answer it. When he came back outside, he sat down and said, "Guess who that was? Dr. Brown."

"Really?" I said, and cautiously asked, "What did he have to say?"

"Ahh, not much. But he said he wants me to try some vitamins and minerals. And he also told me he can give me pain meds and something for sleep when I need it. He's a real nice guy. So glad you got to meet him."

After that phone call, I was confident that Dr. Brown wasn't ready to give up on Art and that he was still going to be there for Art no matter what the prognosis showed.

As we continued to enjoy overlooking Lewis Bay, I noticed a Hy-Line ferry heading out to the islands, making its way to Nantucket or Martha's Vineyard. Then I saw something special—a sailboat in the distance with a big black cat emblazoned on its sail. I said, "Oh, Art, look at that beautiful sailboat. Wouldn't it be fun to go on it?"

He replied, "You know that you can; that's the Cat Boat. It's a commercial sailboat for tourists docked right down the street at Hyannis Harbor."

It felt like it was the perfect thing to do to raise our spirits from the last night's conversation. Almost jumping out of my chair, I said, "Let's do it!"

"Nah, not today…maybe some other time," Art quietly responded.

So I let it go. Art slowly got up and headed inside. He seemed to be fighting pain but did not complain. He was content to sit in his recliner, watch a baseball game, and take a nap. This was to become the new norm for Art in the days ahead.

On Sunday, I packed my stuff and prepared to leave for my drive back home.

Art looked at me and said, "Are you having fun here on the Cape? Why don't you stay until Monday morning? You'll get an extra day here and you'll miss the traffic."

I didn't answer right away but thought to myself, *Am I having fun knowing you're dying? Hell no!* I knew I couldn't say that, so I thought about it for another minute and replied, "No, I'd like to do that, but I really need to get home and be ready for my job on Monday."

"OK," he said. "But think about it; you could have an extra day at the Cape."

I left that afternoon, and as I cried my way home, I vowed that the next weekend when I came back, I would stay the extra day and that on Monday mornings, I would commute to my job from the Cape. And that's what I did every weekend thereafter.

CHAPTER EIGHT

I was so proud of myself when I learned how to make a three-way conference call on my home phone, making it easier to keep in touch with my sisters on a weekly basis. Only the week before during a sisters phone call, Eileen told Charlotte and me that she had a conversation with her husband, Lou, about Art. She told Lou she needed to be a part of helping Art. Lou said to her, "Why do you feel you need to be there with your brother when he hasn't really been a big part of your life for fifteen years?"

She had replied, "Because he's my brother."

Lou had answered, "OK, go for it. If it means that much to you, I'll do anything I can to help."

And so Eileen and I began to split the week spending time with Art. We tried planning our time at the Cape so Art would only be alone a minimum amount of time. I arrived on Friday mornings and stayed until early Monday mornings, when I left for my commute back to work in Connecticut. Eileen came a little later on Monday and stayed for a few days at a time. Although Eileen and I knew that we would mostly not cross paths or see each other, we had a plan. We were going to be there for Art. In the meantime, we kept Charlotte in the loop each week with our sisters conference call. We knew her heart was with us, but we also knew that she was busy preparing for her long-awaited three-week trip to Europe, which was coming up soon. We encouraged Charlotte to stay home and do what she needed to do. We knew this is what Art would want for her, as he never wanted to be a burden to anyone, and especially wouldn't have wanted to take her away from something fun.

Each week, Friday mornings came quickly, and it was already time to pack my car and head to the Cape. This time, I was excited to make the two-and-a-half-hour drive in my new, cute little two-door Honda Accord. Well, it was not brand new, but new to me. I loaded my cooler, my blue-and-yellow-striped duffle bag, and my beach bag into the trunk. This was going to be my test of driving a stick shift long distance. It was a beautiful sunny day, so I cracked the two front windows, slid back the sunroof, put my favorite oldies station on the radio, and headed out on the now-familiar route. I had it memorized: I-84 East toward Sturbridge, then merge onto I-90 East toward Boston. By the time I made it to I-495 South, I found my mind wandering about Art and his life at the Cape.

For some reason, as I rode along, I tried to remember the places Art had worked. I thought about how Art had been part of the restaurant and bar industry in the Hyannis area for over 10 years and how much he loved living and working there. I tried to recall how Art had found his way to the Cape. I knew that for several years, he had skied on weekends at Mt. Snow in Vermont with his wife, Marcia, and their high school friends, the Chernocks and the Barneys. I recalled that skiing was not for Marcia, and she stopped going to Vermont. Art continued to ski on weekends whenever he could. It was in Vermont that Jackie Chernock introduced Art to John Morgan. John owned the popular North Country Fair, an après-ski night spot near Mt. Snow, where he was the sought-after lounge entertainer who could draw hundreds of people on a Saturday night. Art and John became fast friends, and John hired him to work weekends. Art learned to bartend, and he loved it. As they say, "the rest is history."

I remembered that it wasn't long before Art and Marcia's relationship fell apart, and they divorced and parted ways.

I asked myself again, "So how did Art get to the Cape?"

I knew that Art made friends with a whole new crowd of people, and for several years, he skied and worked winters at Mt. Snow and played and worked at John's other nightclub, Pufferbellies, at the Cape in the summers. This group of fun-loving friends may have been the original "reverse snowbirds." It was at the end of one of these summers that Art decided to stay at the Cape year-round.

I smiled when I remembered visiting him when he first moved permanently to the Cape. There he was in his Hawaiian shirt and flip-flops, selling time-shares in Falmouth by day and tending the bar at Pufferbellies by night. I could see that working in a resort town was a perfect match. Art had always enjoyed the beach and especially living near the water. I couldn't help feeling that he had found his new home and living at the Cape would be the life for him.

I continued to reminisce and try to piece together Art's work history at the Cape. I knew that Art, being Art, quickly made connections in the restaurants and bars in the Hyannis area. He once told me that it was easy for him to pick up a shift or two bartending at The Elks Club or at private parties.

Art soon became manager of the legendary Mildred's Chowder House, a position he held for several years. I remembered that during that time, he had also bartended at Howard Johnson's Restaurant and Bar on Main Street in Hyannis, which is where he met his second wife, Heather. I could only imagine how much fun that was for the two of them, working behind the bar together, as they both had a great sense of humor and loved what they did.

Eventually, Art became the full-time general manager at Pufferbellies. He helped his friend John Morgan grow the business to the icon that it soon became, entertaining crowds of people on a Saturday night.

As I drove along, my mind wandered when I thought about how during the summer months, jobs were plentiful in the hospitality industry, but that it must not have been easy to piece together a steady income in the offseason, especially in the dead of winter in a beach vacation area like the Cape. I wondered how that had played out in raising three boys in a stepfamily with both Art and Heather working in the same industry.

Before I knew it, I was crossing over the Sagamore Bridge, which was always one of my favorite parts of driving to the Cape. I loved catching a glimpse of Cape Cod Canal with the sun reflecting in the water and seeing the wake of the boats speeding by. I realized that I was almost there, and reality began to set in.

It was now the end of June, and the summer season at Cape Cod was in full swing. Although Art's health was slowly declining, he kept working, albeit less frequently.

Art continued to place the food and beverage orders for the restaurant for the week and created the shift schedule for the staff. His boss, John Morgan, and his coworkers at Pufferbellies knew his situation, and they knew how much he wanted to keep working. The employees did everything they could to help him cover the staffing needs of the restaurant and filled in for him whenever he needed their help. The word spread that Art was slowing down. His friends rallied around him and dropped by his apartment more often. I got to know several of them on my weekend visits. Art's friends became my friends too. Lulu, one of Art's closest female friends, told me how on several nights that summer, when Art was feeling up to it, he stopped by the Dockside Restaurant where she worked as a bartender. He sat at the end of the service bar sipping his favorite Captain Morgan and Coke while he unfolded and stacked wet dollar bills she received as tips. When anyone asked LuLu why Art was allowed to sit there and they couldn't, she told me that she answered, "Because he's my accountant." LuLu also told me that whenever she had a free evening, she would visit Art after work and would sometimes stay overnight just to keep him company.

Heather came back into Art's life, and even though they were recently divorced, she visited often. They had a good relationship and had remained friends. I noticed that Art always got a twinkle in his eye whenever Heather was around. They really "got" each other. One time when I was arriving for the weekend, Heather and I crossed paths as she was leaving from just having visited Art. With tears in her eyes, she gave me a big hug, which of course made me cry too. She handed me a paper with her home and work number at Kerrigan's and told me to call her anytime. As we said our goodbyes, she said, "Remember, I'm in it for the long haul too."

Things were falling into place to support Art. He also had a special female friend, Linda Brick. She was not a romantic girlfriend but a loyal "girl" friend. Linda and Art had met at Pufferbellies a couple of years earlier and became dear friends. She was straight up honest with Art, and he loved it. Being between jobs that summer, Linda was able to spend a lot of time with Art, popping in on him frequently. On one of my visits, as I got to know her better, we exchanged phone numbers and promised to keep in touch.

"Thanks for being there for Art. It means so much to us that you are looking in on him when we're not here," I said.

"I'm in this for the ride no matter what the outcome is going to be. Call me anytime," she cheerfully replied. As we hugged goodbye, I felt a sense of relief. I knew I could trust Linda to be there for Art and that she was going to be one of "Artie's Angels."

CHAPTER NINE

When Art was well, he almost never cooked meals for himself at home. He would much rather stop at one of his favorite local eateries and have a meal and a cocktail and enjoy the camaraderie at the bar. He could often be found sitting on a barstool at The Mooring, The Dockside, or Spanky's at Hyannis Harbor. He once told me, "Living here is like being on vacation all the time. What's better than eating out?"

When Art lost his appetite and continued to lose weight, I went on a mission to try to keep him nourished. Each week, I brought a meal of his choice. We decided to celebrate the holidays—one weekend, Thanksgiving, with a complete roast turkey breast dinner, and the next weekend, Easter, with ham, sweet potato casserole, and even pumpkin pie. At some point, I must have thought, *If I can just keep him eating, he'll be OK.* Yet deep down, I think we both knew that he would not make it to another actual holiday.

As Art started to eat less and less, I had another brilliant idea: let's try Ensure! I took a chance that he would try it and brought a supply with me on my next weekend visit. So with fingers crossed,

I sheepishly asked him, "How do you feel about trying Ensure? It has plenty of vitamins and helps to boost your energy."

He rolled his eyes and said, "Isn't that for old people?"

I replied, "Yes, it can be, but I thought we might as well give it a try."

He shrugged his shoulders and said, "OK, Marylin, if it will make you happy, let's do it." So I poured him a glass of vanilla-flavored Ensure and he took a sip.

He made a face and said, "Yuck, this stuff is awful."

I then poured him some chocolate-flavored Ensure and waited while he tasted it.

"Oh my God, that's even worse," he winced, trying to wipe it from his lips.

"OK," I said. "You're the mixologist. Let's use your bartender skills and try to make a cocktail with this stuff."

We made our way to the counter that divided the dining room and kitchen, where he sat on a tall stool and I set up our bar. I gathered all the potential ingredients I could find: juice, an assortment of fruit, ice cubes, and even cherries. I put a dish towel over my arm like a waiter and said, "So, Mr. Bartender, what do you suggest?"

He thought for a moment and replied, "Try some pineapple juice."

Luckily, we had a fresh pineapple. I mushed it up and made it as juicy as I could while he watched with a grin on his face. I added it to the Ensure. Since we were now at our makeshift bar, I put my new concoction in a shot glass and waited for him to taste it.

Before he tried it, Art looked at me over the top of his glasses and said, "Well, where's yours?"

This began our taste testing. We clinked glasses, said "Cheers," and downed the pineapple shots.

We each make a face and as I shook my head, I said, "Yuck."

"You're the one that wanted to try this," he said, laughing.

After several more mixtures and more shots, we decided that not coconut milk, orange juice, fruit, or yogurt made it taste any better.

Finally, Art said, "Jesus Christ, this stuff is awful."

"You win," I said. "I agree; it is pretty awful."

Oh well. We had tried. If nothing else, we had a few laughs and had made a new memory for me to hold on to.

CHAPTER TEN

I t was during my weekend visits to Cape Cod that I formed a friendship with Art's landlords, Alice and Bob. They had a lovely brick-front ranch-style home on a small cul-de-sac street where Art rented the apartment over their two-car attached garage. The backyard bordered a wide creek, which flowed in and out to Lewis Bay depending upon the tides. Both Alice and Bob loved to garden. He mowed the lawn and trimmed the shrubs, and she kept the flower gardens weeded and groomed. Although the yard was serene and peaceful, I preferred the beautiful upstairs view of the bay from Art's balcony.

Arriving for my weekly visit on a balmy, cloudless day, I parked my car, and as I rounded the side of the house, I heard the whir of a motor and then saw Bob on his bright green-and-yellow John Deere tractor. We exchanged smiles and I extended my arm in the air with a wave as I yelled, "Hello, Bob!" over the mower noise. Alice was nearby on her knees, digging in the soil, and when I got closer to her, I announced, "I'm back again. Another beautiful day on Cape Cod."

"It sure is! So good to see you," she said as she wiped her hands on her apron.

I stopped to admire the colorful ring of flowers that encircled a small white birch tree in the middle of the yard. "Alice, how do you keep these flowers looking so good?" I asked.

She waved her hand away as if to dismiss the compliment and replied, "Oh, they're just dwarf snapdragons, but here's my secret: plant them in early summer, let them get established and bloom once. Then cut them all the way back and they will bloom for you all summer long."

"Thanks, I'll remember that," I said.

To this day, I have held on to Alice's secret and think of her every year with fond memories when I plant dwarf snapdragons in my own garden.

Alice looked at me with caring eyes and asked, "How's he doing? Can we do anything?"

My usual reply was to take a deep breath and say, "He's OK, thanks for asking." But this time, I couldn't hold the tears back and the words fell out. "Art's doctor told him that the chemo treatments are not working."

Alice got up, stepped forward, and put her arms around me, "Oh, my dear," she said. "He is so lucky to have his sisters visit him so often. Come downstairs anytime you need to...I'll always be here."

From that day on, Alice's kitchen was to become my refuge. Their kitchen door was just across the breezeway from the stairs leading to Art's apartment. Each time I entered or left, I tried to guess what she was cooking. It always smelled so good, like homemade soup or something she was baking. After that conversation, I often took the opportunity to knock on their screen door just to say hello.

"Well," I said, as I paused a moment to gather myself. "It's time to go check on my favorite guy." So upstairs I went, anxious to see Art and begin my weekend.

As I watched Art begin to decline, there were times when my emotions got the best of me. Sometimes I even made an excuse to get something out of my car, check the mailbox, or simply go for a walk. Down the stairs I went, knocked on the kitchen door, and had a good cry with Alice. But sometime during each weekend visit, he never failed to ask, "Are you having fun?"

I would answer, "Sure, Art, you know I love being here." I knew that he didn't want to be a burden, and he so wanted me to enjoy being at the Cape—the Cape he had grown to love.

Art retreated more and more to his favorite brown leather recliner, positioned so that he could watch TV with ease. He loved watching sports, especially baseball. I think baseball was his favorite, as he had played from the time he was in Little League and went on to be a great athlete in high school, lettering in baseball, basketball, and football. He slept more, ate less, and wasn't up for a lot of conversation. I continued to try and find things that might pique his dwindling appetite. I used my best Martha Stewart skills to artfully arrange a small plate with fresh fruit, cheese, nuts, and crackers, which I placed on a small table beside his chair in hopes that he'd find something appealing. "Here you go, Mr. Westfall, at your service. Anything else I can get for you?" I asked while holding my imaginary skirt and bowing in a playful curtsy.

"Ahh, thanks. You didn't have to make it so fancy. Maybe I'll have some later."

After a few weekends of making my snack plates, I noticed that I was on automatic pilot, preparing almost the same snacks and taking away the same dish at the end of the day with dried cheese, stale crackers, and limp fruit. My strategy was not working.

In my weekly call with my sister Eileen, I asked her how her visits were going to see if she had any better ideas of what we could do to feed and take care of Art.

"How are you doing on your watch?" I asked.

"Well, here's what happened on my visit this week," she offered. "I've been trying to care of his toe, the one that's turning black and blue. Did you notice that it's the only thing he's complaining about? Poor guy." She went on to say, "I'm so frustrated that the doctor doesn't seem to be doing anything to ease the toe pain or find out what it is. I guess it's not a priority at this stage of the game, but it's so hard to see him in such pain." She began to cry, and through her tears, she sobbed, "I don't know what to do or how to help him."

"I know, I know," I consoled her, "but we're doing the best we can."

She blew her nose and continued, "I'm trying to keep his toe clean by gently cleaning it with a Q-tip and putting on some antibacterial ointment. Yesterday, I brought out my nurse's kit, and when I opened a clear round container of one hundred and fifty Q-tips, he looked at me, winked, and said with a grin, "I don't think I'll be needing all of those,"

Now, we both cried.

By mid-July, Art was not going to work at Pufferbellies anymore and had unofficially taken a leave of absence. I think he had hoped that he might feel better and be able to go back to work, or at least pick up an occasional shift. He settled into his recliner, only getting up to use the bathroom or take an occasional walk to the balcony. But falling asleep in his recliner became a problem that I had to address. Art was a smoker. He smoked Marlboros in his nonsmoking apartment. I worried what his landlords would do if they found out. Would they ask him to leave? Did they already know? I became more and more concerned for his safety when I noticed cigarette ashes on the floor and burn holes in the orange-and-gold crocheted throw that he tossed over his legs while he napped. I finally mustered up all my courage and said, "Art, you can't smoke in your chair anymore. You're beginning to fall asleep with a lit cigarette, and I'm afraid you'll burn the place down." I felt terrible, as it was one of the few pleasures he had left. I knew he had to stop, or at least he could no longer smoke in his recliner. He replied sheepishly, as though he knew it was coming, "OK, I know, I know, if that's what you want."

Art actually stopped smoking. When I look back, I almost think he forgot to smoke. This was the beginning of him letting go of life as he had known it.

CHAPTER ELEVEN

Near the end of July, Art's friends slowly began to visit less. One of them told me they knew he was resting a lot and that we, his sisters, were there taking good care of him. However, many did keep in touch with cards and notes. One day when I went to Art's mailbox, there was an envelope addressed to the Westfall sisters from "Kelly." This letter was a total surprise, as at that time, Art didn't seem to have any significant girlfriend. It was unusual for him not to have a woman in his life, being the ladies' man that he was, but I never questioned it...until the letter came.

Here's what Kelly wrote:

Dear Charlotte, Marylin, and Eileen,

I won't say that I am sorry about Artie, but I am greatly saddened. I would not have traded the time with him for anything in the world. Never has anyone touched my life the way Art did, and I'm sure that no one else will ever do so again.

I hope you don't mind one more person sharing some memories with you and showing again what a truly remarkable man that Artie is.

I met Artie at the Harbor House three years ago. From the first time I saw him sitting at the bar, I knew there was something about him that I liked instantly and knew it wasn't just that he always smelled so good! I'm not a shy person, yet it took me from April until the end of May to get the courage to sit next to him. In the meantime, Artie had asked a couple of people about me, then I guess he figured because I wasn't trying to make conversation with him, "Forget her, she's a snob." Lucky for me, I did get the nerve to talk to him. We hit it off instantly, found we had a lot in common, and shared many of the same interests.

I had left an abusive marriage three years previously. Artie instinctively knew this and went out of his way (not that he of all people needed to) to show me that there are men who are not assholes. I was amazed at his attitude toward all women. He had such respect and admiration for women. I couldn't figure out where this came from.

Since we both worked such long hours, our favorite nights "out" became curling up on the couch with each other and relaxing. It was during one of these nights that I learned why he thought women were the strongest and most beautiful creatures God had ever made. As we sat

on the couch that night, I was rubbing his hands as I
had done on several occasions previously. He asked why
I was rubbing his hands and I told him I loved the feel
of his hands, so warm and soft, and that they seemed
to reflect the person to whom they belonged. I thought
maybe it bothered him that I rubbed his hands, and
he quickly assured me that it didn't. He then shared
a beautiful story about five wonderful women in his
life—his mother, his Grandma Fern, and his three sisters.

Art told me that he was grateful and that he knew
that he wouldn't be the person he was without these
women. He told me of his early years of abuse by his
father, both physically and emotionally. He told me
how his grandmother used to sit and rub his hands for
hours and assure him that he was a good and beautiful
person and how loved he was. He also told me of a
wonderful mother and her courage and strength to get
through life. He shared how grateful he was that Gus,
his stepfather, had been such a caring person in her life.

He then told me about "the girls." How surrounded
by love and affection he had always felt from each of
you. He considered himself one of the luckiest men in
the world to have all of you as a part of him.

He showed such courage and strength from the
start of all of this and has never wavered.

I wanted to share a little bit more that you may
or may not know by now. Artie knew just how serious

everything was since last May (1995). He made me promise not to say anything to John Morgan, his friend and boss, or anyone else, because he was worried about all of you and didn't think it was fair to have you deal with this so soon after your mother's death.

Through the next nine months, I spent the majority of nights with Artie, and he would talk for hours about how worried he was for "the girls" and how you would handle everything. He said as long as he thought you would be OK, then he was OK. Never once did he curse fate or feel sorry for himself. Only on a few occasions while we were both having a good cry did he even admit how scared he was. Then he would immediately apologize, say he shouldn't burden me with this, and that he was sorry, but he felt like he needed to talk to someone. Artie meant a lot to me, and burden is never a word I would associate with him. I had a tragic death in my family in January, and Artie was right there for me despite all he was dealing with himself.

I had a conversation with Art in February in which he wanted me to promise him that I wouldn't be around all the time at the end because he felt I had done too much for him already and that in the next few months, he would be OK and that he would lean on family and friends for support. He also understood that I couldn't just walk away. A month later, he did the only mean thing I've ever seen him do, which was not mean at all but a very selfless act.

We usually went out on Sunday nights. On this night, I couldn't figure out what was wrong with him. From the time he picked me up, he was not himself. I thought he was having a bad day, so I didn't say anything. He was rude, made insulting comments about my outfit (which I knew he had liked before), flirted outrageously with another woman, and continued making insulting remarks throughout the evening. I finally snapped on the ride home, when at this point, out of desperation and frustration, he insulted my kids. I finally blew and told him to go to hell.

Two days later, and after many hours of thinking, I called him and said, "I know what you did, Mr. Westfall."

He laughed and said, "I thought it would take forever when you didn't get upset sooner," and that he realized that that was the one thing that would get me.

Artie and I continued to talk on the phone over the next few months and remain good friends. He would occasionally stop in, and we would have tea together and talk for hours.

Artie enjoyed every day of life and could find something beautiful in each one. He also gave me a gift that I will cherish and never lose or let anyone take away from me again. He showed me that I don't have to be perfect, but not to settle for anyone who doesn't treat me as if I am.

Art had a way with people. He made you feel a part of him and he a part of you.

Thank you all for letting me share these thoughts with you. I will remember all of you often and keep you in my prayers.

Kelly

I wept when I finished reading this heartfelt letter and couldn't wait to share it with my sisters. I knew I could not share it with Art, which broke my heart. I put on my sneakers and windbreaker and headed to the beach for a cry. On my way out, I must have startled him, as Art woke up from dozing and said, "Hey, are you having fun? You know that I want you to have fun when you're at the Cape."

"Sure," was all that I could manage to say. I was as upbeat as I could manage to be. "I'm headed out for a walk on the beach."

I turned my head away so that he could not see the tears running down my face. With my heart breaking after reading Kelly's letter, I thought to myself, *Sure Art; I'm having fun knowing that you're dying.*

CHAPTER TWELVE

After reading the heartfelt letter from Art's girlfriend Kelly, I couldn't get to the beach quick enough. I ran down the cut-through path to the little beach at the end of Art's street, pushing the branches aside and wiping tears as I went. I was so grateful it was late afternoon and the beach was mostly empty. It was a perfect day with a gentle sea breeze and a beautiful cloudless blue sky. My heart was hurt thinking of Art's condition, something I hadn't really wanted to admit even to myself: he was in the late stages of pancreatic cancer.

When I reached the warm sand, I kicked off my flip-flops, and since it was low tide, I waded across the creek. I walked along the water's edge past Veterans Memorial Park and crossed the boardwalk at Hyannis Yacht Club. My mind racing with so many thoughts of Art and our life growing up together, I found myself also wading down memory lane.

I thought of all the years the four of us, the Westfall kids, clung together to get through life. I thought of how being children of an abusive alcoholic father, we took care of each other the best we could. I shuddered as I remembered how I slept with a pillow over my head and blankets pulled up over my ears to drown out the disruptive noises of the night. A vision flashed before my eyes. I saw the many nights when our father was exceptionally drunk and abusive. I remembered how our mother was the main target of the almost nightly abuse, both physically and mentally. I thought about how Ma did everything she could to try to keep him quiet so we could get a good night's sleep and be able to go to school the next day. I remembered we often did not have a home phone, or at least one that was paid up and connected. So when our father was exceptionally out of control and abusive, Charlotte, the oldest sibling, took it upon herself to run to the pay phone booth on the corner of our street to call the police. It happened frequently enough that most of the local police officers knew him by name. When they arrived, one of us would let them in. The police officers would go upstairs to our parents' bedroom and I'd hear them say, "Come on, Charlie, we're going to take you in for the night." He'd try to talk them out of taking him by faking sleep and then saying, "What do ya mean, officer? I was just about to go to sleep." Thankfully, they would take him to the police station for the night, only to have him sweet-talk his way back into the house the next day. These are the memories that I would rather forget.

As I kept walking along the water's edge, I thought about how as youngsters, we walked a long distance, at least a mile or two, to church and back, even though neither of our parents ever went with us. I recalled that sometimes we each had a dime or a token to take the bus one way, either to church or on the way home. I smiled when I remembered how we often played a game along the way: *Let's keep walking, and if we make it all the way to church, we'll spend the money at the penny candy store on the way home. Or if the bus doesn't come on our way there, then we'll be able to take it on the way home.*

I continued to walk along, picking up shells and aimlessly searching for sea glass. I smiled when I remembered that Charlotte had once bought the four of us brand new Halloween costumes. Since we had never had a costume from a store, we were thrilled.

She must have been about twelve and used her babysitting money to take two buses to Bridgeport to make her surprise purchase. That year, Art was a cowboy, I was a majorette with a sparkly baton, Eileen was a cowgirl, and I think Charlotte was a gypsy. Oh, how we loved those costumes!

I seemed to be in a daze as I continued to walk, and my mind continued to wander. I remembered a time when Art was about seven years old. He was playing in the swamp across the street from our house and got stuck in quicksand. The more we tried to pull him out, the further his boots got stuck in the muck. After trying to use branches to pry him out, I held on to him while Charlotte ran home to get an old shovel and we shoveled him out! Oh my; what a memory.

My mind kept racing, recalling how Art, at about nine or ten years old, got his first baseball glove. Our Uncle Johnny was visiting us from West Virginia with his family of nine children. One afternoon while he played catch with a baseball with Art, something our father never took the time to do, he said, "Got quite an arm there, kid; I think you're going to be a good ball player."

Art loved the encouragement and beamed as he said, "Thanks, Uncle Johnny, you really think so?"

To Art's surprise and delight, the next day, Uncle Johnny, of little means but a huge heart, went to a store and bought Art his first real baseball glove. Art never disappointed him…he became a good baseball player. Somehow Art managed to find a ride to and from his games and practices since our family did not have a car most of the time. The times when we did have a car, our father had little interest in Art playing baseball and could not to be counted on to drive him. Although our mother could give the best directions to most anywhere, she never got her driver's license. We kids were on our own to find rides with friends to wherever we wanted to go.

I kept walking along the water's edge, sinking into the wet sand and enjoying the waves lapping at my knees. The memories just kept coming. I found myself at a bittersweet place that I never really liked to go. I thought of the time when we finally left our father and moved across town. I recalled how we managed to make it happen…Charlotte was then a year out of high school, working full-time at a bank and planning her wedding. She made the calls, found the rental, and took part of the money that she was saving for her wedding to pay the first month's rent on a two-bedroom duplex house across town. Grandma Fern, who was our father's mother and had always lived with us, came too. She had often been our sole financial support and continued to clean houses and take in ironing. I was a senior in high school and contributed what I could from my part-time job working as a checkout clerk at the A&P grocery store. I remembered that two months later, the morning after I graduated from high school, I started a full-time job as a secretary at a local manufacturing company. I was then able to take over paying the family's monthly rent. Our mother eventually got a steady job as a waitress, working at W. T. Grant's lunch counter. Of course, she had to take two public buses to get there. When we made the move, Art and Eileen were still in elementary school. Eileen chose to take two buses to complete eighth grade in her old school, and Art walked to the new neighborhood school for seventh and eighth grade. We still had no car, but it almost didn't matter as none of us could drive. We were on a public bus line, which was a short walk up the street, and we were determined to make this move work.

I was glad that I had grabbed a pocketful of tissues as I found myself crying, yet sometimes smiling, as memories continued to come alive. I thought about when I was a teenager and used to take Art on dates with me. On Saturday nights, my steady boyfriend, Dick, often came over to spend time at our house. Art, who was now about twelve, would always be hanging around. Sometimes Dick and I had plans to go out to a movie or bowling. I often felt sorry for Art and would ask Dick if it would be OK if Art came on our date, and many times he did.

Before I knew it, a new memory came: *What about the sneakers?* That was one of my saddest memories. When Art was in high school and I was now out in the working world, I bought him his first pair of high-top Converse sneakers. They were all the rage and I wanted him to have them. I was so happy to be able to do that for him. He was thrilled and couldn't thank me enough. A week later, he came home from school and told me that the sneakers had been stolen from his locker. I think we cried together.

I stopped to sit on a big rock. I inhaled the smell of the salt water and stared out at the bay, taking in the seagulls circling overhead. But my mind would not be quiet. Still another memory of Art came to me. When I married Dick, Art was only fifteen, but he was my choice to walk me down the aisle. He looked so handsome and grown-up in his tux...such a fond memory.

I'm not sure why the wedding memory brought me to thinking about our father, as he had passed by this time at the young age of forty-two years old. Unfortunately he died penniless and in squalor at the home of an elderly couple who lived across the street from the house that we had left him in. I tried to remember just why our father didn't have a steady job. And why didn't we always have a car?

I knew that he had worked when we first came to Connecticut, but that at some point, I believe he had accidentally gotten a piece of steel in his finger, triggering blood poisoning, and was out of work for a time. He only seemed to work intermittently and drank more. He had been in and out of the Veterans Hospital and was eventually diagnosed with scleroderma and Raynaud's disease, which both have to do with small blood vessels of the extremities. He had the tips of several fingers removed due to the scleroderma tightening the skin and lack of circulation and was in a lot of pain, especially during the cold months. All of a sudden, I had a flash memory of how he had once even converted a tropical fish tank with a light bar into a warming station and would sit with his hands in it and cry in pain. I hadn't thought about this in years and realized what a complex issue it must have been for us kids, wanting to love and have empathy for him and not being able to because of the alcoholic abuse. He even tried bartending but could not stand handling the cold drinks and ice cubes. As I looked back, I also remembered that he had old hearing aids, which really didn't work, and a pair of used eyeglasses. While I couldn't excuse his behavior, my heart hurt when I considered what it must have been like for him as a man who I don't think could read or write—and as a man who could not provide for his family. Even today, when I write about this, it breaks my heart to think there was no way of saving him and that he died in such an awful place at such a young age.

The sun was getting lower in the sky when I realized that I'd walked a long way and decided I had better turn around and get back to Art's apartment. Now the wind was at my back, pushing me along as I continued to pick up shells and hunt for a treasured piece of sea glass.

Arriving back at Art's place, Alice, his landlord, was working in her flower gardens. I stopped for a short visit. She could see that I had been crying and asked with concern, "How's your brother doing?"

I paused and could only quietly get out, "He's OK." As always, she stood up and gave me a hug. She softly said, "Remember, if there's ever anything we can do, don't hesitate to ask."

"Ahh, thanks Alice," I said. "So good to know that you and Bob are here."

I took a deep breath, pulled myself together, and headed back upstairs to check on Art. Arriving at the top of the steps to his apartment, I was thrilled to see him up and moving about. "Well, I did it again," I said as cheerfully as I could.

He replied, "Did what again?"

"Picked up a pocketful of shells."

He playfully chuckled and said, "Why don't you just leave them there?"

"I guess the same reason that you pick up little treasures when you walk the water's edge," I answered.

He laughed and gave me a wink. "You're right. Have you seen my treasures?"

He took me by the hand and we walked across the room to a glass-enclosed bookcase. On one of the shelves was a large brandy snifter filled with his beach finds: a matchbox truck, a wooden nickel, a small red-haired troll doll, and a rubber lobster, to name a few. We had a great laugh. I still have Art's treasures, saved in a plastic storage box, each individually wrapped with loving care by Eileen.

"Hey," he said. "My friends called and want to come over next Friday to talk about setting up a charitable foundation to benefit hospitality workers on the Cape. You know, like the fundraiser they did for me. Will you be here?"

"Sure, I would love to see your friends. How about I make

something, like a dessert?" I immediately replied.

"OK, that would be great. Can you make my favorite?"

"What's that?" I asked.

"Pineapple upside-down cake," he replied.

"You're on," I answered.

Looking forward to having this meeting seemed to raise both of our spirits. He put his arm around me, and we walked to his balcony to enjoy the evening view. The sun was just beginning to set, casting its orange-and-gold reflection on the water in the distance. As I looked down to the driveway below, I noticed Alice and Bob putting away their gardening tools. Art saw them too and called out to them, "Beautiful evening, how are you guys doing?"

They looked up, surprised to see us on the balcony, and Alice replied, "Great, Art. How are you?"

"Not bad for a guy with a bad toe," he replied.

Alice and Bob glanced at each other, gave a little chuckle, and let it go.

"Oh, by the way, I've been meaning to tell you," Art called down, "I won't be needing the apartment after this month. OK if we just use my last month's rent to finish the lease?"

My heart dropped. Alice and Bob were silent. I think they were trying to take in what he had just said. Finally, after what seemed like hours, Alice looked up with tears in her eyes and said, "Sure, Art. That will be fine."

"OK, then. Have a good night," he replied, just like it was any other day.

Feeling numb, I put one foot in front of the other and walked back inside with Art. *What to say? What to do?* I had no words and neither did he.

Art settled back into his recliner, pulled up his throw, and said to me, "You know Marylin, I think this would be a great place for you to rent. Why don't you think about it?"

"Sure, Art, I'll think about it," was all that I could say.

CHAPTER THIRTEEN

After another busy week of trying to keep my mind at work and my job intact, I packed the car for my drive to the Cape to be with Art for another weekend. I had even managed to find time to make his favorite dessert, pineapple upside-down cake. The aroma of yellow sheet cake still filled the kitchen. The pineapple slices were perfectly arranged in three rows across the cake, each topped with a bright red maraschino cherry and covered with a brown sugar glaze. I had also added pecan halves here and there, hoping to give it a gourmet look. I was so pleased with my efforts; the cake turned out great. Now that it was cooled, I covered it with foil and packed it carefully in a copy paper box for the drive to Hyannis.

My car was beginning to know the way on its own, as the weekly drive to the Cape had become a familiar routine. Before I knew it, once again, I crossed the Sagamore Bridge and enjoyed the view as I savored the sun's reflection on the water of the Cape Cod Canal below. As I got closer to my destination, my thoughts turned to what lay ahead. *How will Art be this time? What can I do to make these days special? Am I going to be able to handle whatever comes?* I felt a pang of sadness as I passed by Pufferbellies on my right. I thought of all the years that Art had worked there and how it had truly become his happy place. I took a deep breath and attempted to get myself together. *You can do this*, I told myself as I prepared for our weekly visit. I passed by Hyannis Harbor and another wave of sorrow hit me. This was Art's playground. All the restaurants and bars that he loved. *OK, Marylin, now you really have to get it together.* Art's street was coming up on the left.

I parked my car in the usual spot on the apron of the driveway behind the garage, gathered my things, and headed for the stairs to Art's apartment.

"Hello, dear," I heard as I passed by Alice and Bob's open kitchen door. "Here for the weekend, are you?"

"Oh, yes I am, Alice, and how are you?"

She stepped outside and said, "Couldn't be better on this lovely day."

"By the way," I said. "A group of Art's friends will be coming by this afternoon. If they look lost, will you just send them upstairs? And guess what? I made a special dessert for the gathering. I'll bring down a piece for you and Bob when they have gone."

"That would be wonderful, we'll look forward to it. Now, don't forget that if you need anything, don't hesitate to ask."

My arms were full, but she was able to reach around and give me a hug before I headed up the stairs.

"Thanks, Alice," I whispered in her ear. "I'll be down later."

When I got to the top of the stairs, I was greeted by Art's dear friend, Linda.

"Hey, Sister #2, I was hoping we would cross paths today," she said as she took the box with the cake from me. "Now, what's in this yummy-smelling box?"

"Oh, that's a surprise for today's meeting. Are you staying?" I answered.

She replied, "No, but let me help you bring in the rest of your stuff."

I had only met Linda in person a couple times but had talked with her several times on the phone. She was a tall, trim blonde in her early forties who carried herself with a confident air and a zest for life. I later found out why; Art told me that Linda had been an Associated Press photographer with exciting and sometimes dangerous assignments. She was hired to photo document US troops in war-torn countries. She once told me she had been dropped many times behind enemy lines with only her camera and a backpack. She had recently left that job and was making a new life for herself at the Cape. That's when she met Art at Puffer-bellies and they had hit it off right away. Linda had agreed to stop by often to spend time with Art and give us peace of mind when we sisters could not be there. Today, she had dropped by until I could get there. Linda was a great addition to our small group of caregivers and Art loved it when she visited. I sensed he could be himself without having to protect her, as he seemed to want to do with us Westfall sisters, or as he referred to us, "the girls."

"Good to see you," she said. "We are usually like two ships passing in the night."

"I know," I said. "So good to see you live in person."

We exchanged unspoken knowing glances, and I wondered what it had been like on her watch.

"Hey," Art shouted from his recliner. "Here she is, one of my favorite redheads."

I crossed the room and almost fell into his recliner as I reached down for a hug.

"And exactly how many redheads do you have?" I replied.

He chuckled and said, "I'll never tell."

"I put his meds in the weekly container, and he has taken the morning ones for today. I have to run, so he's all yours," Linda said as she made her way to the stairs. She stopped to give Art a peck on the cheek and said, "OK, Art, you're in good hands. I'll see you later."

He said, "Thanks, you're the best."

And off she went.

I settled in, putting away the things I had brought for the weekend, including the cake. I reminded Art that today was the day his friends were coming. He remembered and said, "Yes, I know. Do you mind if I take a little nap before they get here?"

"No, not at all. I'll just make myself at home and read for a while on your balcony."

It was not long before I heard them coming up the stairs. Someone playfully shouted, "Where the hell are you, Art Westfall?"

He immediately perked up from dozing and shouted back, "Where the hell did you expect me to be? Come on in, I'm right here relaxing and waiting for you."

Art's face lit up when the group came in the room, including

Debbie Morgan, LuLu Murray, John Shea, Suzy Morgan, and Ed Miles. Each one greeted him with a special hug that seemed to never want to end. When I opened the slider and appeared from the balcony, Art smiled and said, "You all remember my sister, Marylin? She's here to make sure that I behave."

We all laughed and shared more hugs around.

"Welcome, find a seat, everyone," I said. I pushed the sofa in closer, then carried in a couple kitchen chairs and found a seat for everyone until they were all gathered comfortably near Art's recliner. I didn't know where my place in all of this was, so I retreated to the kitchen to keep myself busy and began to prepare the dessert.

"So, let's get started. What have you got so far?" asked Art.

"Well, Art," Debbie said. "We know how much you appreciated the event held for you and that you really wanted to keep this fundraising going, so we are going to start an ongoing fund in your name. If it's okay with you, we'd like to name it "The Art Westfall Fund.""

Art seemed very touched and said, "OK, tell me more."

"We've written a letter that will explain it all. I'll read it," replied Debbie.

To: The Hospitality Industry, Cape Cod, MA

"Men die but once, and the opportunity to die a noble death is not an everyday fortune: it is a gift that noble spirits pray for."

—Charles Lamb

Some people look at death as an opportunity. Many complain, ask why, or ask, How could this happen to me? But some people look at death as an opportunity to live, to love, and to remember all that is well and good. This is Art Westfall.

Last year, after hearing of the terrible fate Artie was given, being diagnosed with a life-threatening cancer, we threw a party, not out of sympathy, but out of the love we all felt deep inside. We wanted to celebrate a life we all loved participating in, a life full of compassion, courage, and friendship. It was a fundraiser to help him with his battle for life. I am sorry to report the battle is nearly over, but his love and compassion are stronger than ever. In the bottom of the ninth inning of life, Artie has requested a committee be formed and a fund started so the efforts that began for him continue for others. We are that committee.

Oh my God, I thought. *What did I just hear?* The letter pronounced that "his battle is nearly over and that he's in the bottom of the ninth inning of life." I turned my back to the group to hide the tears that were uncontrollably flowing. I didn't know what to do. *Did Art just hear that? Did they mean to say that? Do they know that he is sitting right there?* When I got the courage to turn around, I looked over at Art, and for the first time in this whole process, tears were rolling down his cheeks. He pulled his baseball hat down to cover his face. My heart broke for him, but I couldn't move—I was frozen to do anything.

Debbie went on reading a letter the committee had prepared, soliciting sponsors for upcoming fundraisers:

> The Art Westfall Fund is a nonprofit organization to benefit those people in the Hospitality Industry of Cape Cod. The money raised in this fund will be used in the event one of our own falls ill and is in need of assistance. We have decided that our fund will be used for whatever the person wants. It could help pay the everyday cost of living or to take their loved ones on a dream vacation. We are having a golf tournament on September 11 and are looking for hole sponsors. It will cost $50 to sponsor a hole. Information on the tournament is enclosed. Our first fundraiser will be on September 15 at Pufferbellies and information is also enclosed. We will publish a newsletter and report our progress on a regular basis and will be planning other events throughout the year. We hope you will encourage your staff to become involved in this effort. We are looking forward to celebrating a great cause for such tremendous people. Thank you.
>
> Sincerely,
> The Art Westfall Fund Committee
> Debbie Morgan, LuLu Murray, John Shea, Suzy Morgan, Ed Miles, and Artie Westfall

Silence filled the room as each one seemed to take in what had just been read.

After what seemed like an eternity, I finally said, "Well, folks, I made Art's favorite dessert. Who wants a piece of homemade pineapple upside-down cake?"

Everyone breathed a sigh of relief and reached for a piece of cake from my tray. Art lifted his hat and said with a grin, "And she's not a bad cook either."

The group talked about getting a mailing list together of all the local pubs and restaurants. Each took a part of the town to canvas for donations and support. They agreed to meet again to prepare the mailing. Art thanked them all and said, "You guys are the best! This is going to be great!" There were more hugs for Art and me as they said their goodbyes to him, thanked me, and made their way out, holding back the tears that now filled their eyes.

"You take care, Art; we'll be in touch," said Deb Morgan.

"Sure," said Art. "I'll be right here."

After I said goodbye to each one and the room had emptied out, I turned to see Art slumped in his chair as though all the air had gone out of him. I crossed the room, sat on his lap, curled up in his arms, and…we cried.

After a while, Art perked up and said, "Let's check out the balcony; maybe the Cat Boat is going by."

Hand in hand, we made our way to the sliders and walked out onto the balcony. I still felt numb, not wanting to allow the pain I was feeling to escape or leak out. I gazed out to Lewis Bay. Art stared straight ahead too. For a while, neither of us said a word. Art finally broke the silence when he said, "You know, Marylin, I've always wanted to live to be eighty, but right now I'm hoping for fifty." (It was early August, and Art's fiftieth birthday was coming up on September 17.)

I didn't respond.

Art continued to stare out ahead at the bay. "I've been thinking about a Viking funeral. You know, how they used to place the body on a pyre and let it float out to sea."

He turned his head, looked at me, winked, and we both cracked up laughing.

I playfully hit him on the shoulder and said, "Not before we go on that Cat Boat."

CHAPTER FOURTEEN

The weeks continued to go by quickly. After spending each weekend with Art, I drove home from the Cape on Monday mornings, went right to my office, and attempted to do my job. Fortunately, I had been doing this job for many years and I had an understanding boss. I could almost do it with my eyes closed. I pulled it off one more week. It was already Thursday again and time to cook something to take with me on my weekly journey to the Cape. I decided on spaghetti sauce with meatballs, sausage, and braciole. Surely Art would like that! Who wouldn't like our stepfather Gus's authentic Italian sauce? We Westfall siblings were all young adults when Ma married Gus. We had no idea what a good cook he was. I remembered the first time I tasted Gus's sauce at a Sunday family dinner. I took one look at the meat in the sauce and politely passed, not even knowing what it was. After watching the rest of the family devour the braciole, I finally got brave enough to try it. To my delight, it was delicious! I was determined to learn how to make it. Ma agreed to teach me. She even taught me Gus's secrets...he always sprinkled the spices—

minced garlic, parsley, oregano, salt, and pepper—right on top of several very thin strips of flank steak, which I found out you can only buy in an authentic Italian grocery store. Ma showed me how Gus then rolled the steak up jelly roll-style, tied it with thread, and allowed the braciole to simmer in the sauce until it was so tender you could cut it with a fork.

I knew Gus's sauce with pasta was second only to Art's first love, Pepe's Pizza in New Haven, Connecticut. Over the years that Art had lived at the Cape, when any of us visited him, he would always request, "Bring me some Pepe's Pizza!"

The Westfall sisters decided we would make one more sisters' visit to the Cape before Charlotte left for her two-week trip to Europe. Art was so glad to see us and welcomed each of us as we arrived separately for another Westfall sibling weekend. It was a quiet weekend this time, as Art wasn't up to doing much. We mostly just hung out together on Art's balcony, our favorite place to gather to relax and enjoy the view. On Saturday afternoon, as we were enjoying the warm, sunny, beautiful day, Charlotte decided to take this opportunity to teach us how to contact our "angels," which she had just learned when visiting a local angel store. She told us to write a question to your angel with your dominant hand and you will get an answer by writing with your opposite hand. While we all made an attempt at this method by writing our questions on index cards, Art wanted no part of it. He looked over at me, frowned, rolled his eyes in disbelief, and decided to go inside. A few minutes later, Art came out of the bathroom looking white as a ghost. He was agitated with a look of fear on his face.

He asked, "What is he doing here?" We all looked at each other, puzzled, and didn't know who or what he was talking about. As if to protect him, Eileen forcefully said, "Be gone! Go away! You don't belong here."

I wasn't sure what had just happened, but that was the end of trying to contact the angels. We put the index cards away and Art retreated to his recliner for a nap. The rest of us closed our eyes and took a chair nap on the balcony.

When it was almost time for dinner, I made my way into the small kitchen, excited to heat up my homemade sauce with Gus's famous braciole. Eileen set the table with colorful placemats and napkins. Charlotte added a couple candles and arranged the chairs around the table. I hadn't told them what I was bringing for dinner, but as soon as the aroma of Italian spices filled the air, they guessed it.

Eileen said, "Oh my God, did you make Gus's sauce?"

"Yes I did!" I proudly exclaimed.

"Well, good for you, Marylin Kay, we didn't know you knew how to make it," Charlotte said with a touch of jealousy in her voice.

"Ma taught me," I boasted.

Eileen placed a beautiful tossed salad that she had brought from home in the middle of the table. Charlotte had brought garlic bread, which she popped in the oven to heat. Art joined us at the table for our Italian feast. He took one look at the meal and said, "Whoa, thanks. You girls outdid yourselves this time!" I was so hoping that Art might like this meal, but I soon found out that his appetite had continued to dwindle, and he only politely pushed the food around his plate.

I tried not to show my disappointment. It finally dawned on me that loss of appetite might be part of Art's declining health.

After the meal, while we cleared the dishes, Art walked around, pulling down all the shades on the windows and sliders surrounding the room. We looked at each other, again puzzled, and shrugged our shoulders. I was afraid to say anything. What was he doing? It was only six o'clock and still very light outside.

Charlotte said, "Art, what are you doing? It's still beautiful out."

He responded, "Oh, I'm just battening down the hatches."

And she replied, "Well, don't do that. We'll do it later when it gets dark."

"OK," he said, almost like a child who had done something wrong, and headed for his recliner.

I couldn't help but wonder what just happened. Lately I had noticed that Art's behavior seemed to be getting strange and none of us wanted to admit it. I thought to myself, *Is Art's medication beginning to cause confusion? Is his intermittent sleeping pattern beginning to take a toll? What do we do?*

Once again, Charlotte, Eileen, and I headed for the balcony to enjoy the sunset and regroup before preparing to head home. We each had a concerned look on our face and hoped that one of us had an idea of what was going on with Art.

I remembered that Art had a doctor's appointment on Monday, the next day, and I suggested, "What if we just stay for his appointment tomorrow? He's going to need a ride anyway."

We all agreed that it was the right thing to do and settled in for the evening, watching the sun go down. Since Art was already sleeping, we decided not to tell him that we were staying an extra night. We assumed he would be OK with our decision. When he woke up the next morning, Art was pleasantly surprised to see that we were still there. I said, "So, Art, we decided to stay because we want to go to your doctor's appointment with you."

He looked at me with a grin and said, "Sure, suit yourselves. It'll be one big party."

When we arrived at Dr. Brown's office, Art greeted the receptionist with a smile, winked, and said, "These are my sisters. They're my bodyguards."

She laughed and replied, "Lucky you. Have a seat; it won't be long for your appointment."

In a short while, she announced, "It's your turn, Art. Come on in."

He stood, turned, and looked at the three of us, then looked back at the receptionist and said, "They might as well come in too, because if they don't, they will only grill me to the wall with questions." And he gave her another wink.

We followed Art into the office, where Dr. Brown was standing behind a large desk. Art sat down in the chair in front of the desk, and we sat in the chairs by the wall behind him. Dr. Brown said, "Hey, Art, good to see you. Well, who are all these lovely ladies?"

"These are my sisters, Charlotte, Marylin, and Eileen. You might as well tell them everything; it will keep them from twisting my pinky finger to get the information out of me."

"OK," Dr. Brown said with an understanding grin. "Shoot—any questions?"

"Yes," I immediately said. "He's not eating. I try to think of new things all the time. Any suggestions?"

"Yes." Dr. Brown paused for a moment, and in his very soft -spoken and compassionate voice continued, "Don't worry about what he eats or doesn't eat. If he wants something special, jump on it; otherwise let it go. He will know if he's hungry or not."

I put my tail between my legs and sat quietly back in my chair.

Dr. Brown directed his attention to Art, inquiring about his pain, sleep habits, anxiety, and any questions that he might have had. Art sheepishly admitted that he was having a little abdominal pain and that he was not able to sleep on a regular basis. Dr. Brown seemed to sense what was going on and offered a suggestion. "Why don't we do this, Art; let's have a nurse start stopping by your place a few times a week to help you keep up with your meds and pain management. How does that sound?"

Art looked down. His shoulders dropped, he nodded his head slowly in agreement as if he was giving in, and said, "Sure, just send me a pretty one."

Dr. Brown looked directly at Art and said, "Art, you know that we can do something for the pain if it gets too bad. Just say the word."

"You got it," Art said. "Now, I'll just take my harem and let you get on with your day. Thanks, Doc."

We drove Art home, finding little to say. I think we were each trying to process what Dr. Brown had just said…and what he did not say. I silently began to worry. *Will he still be OK on his own a few days at a time? Is leaving him on his own the right thing to do?* I convinced myself it would be OK for now and that his friend Linda and the new nurse would be stopping by to check on him.

After we packed our cars, getting ready to head home, we came back upstairs to take our turns at hugging Art. Charlotte was the last to say goodbye. Art pulled her close and held on to her as if he didn't want to let her go. Little did they both know, that was the last time they would see each other. Or, maybe on some level, they did know.

CHAPTER FIFTEEN

This week, we left Art on his own for a few days. I was worried about him. I had kept in touch with his friend Linda, who had agreed to check on him. She promised that she would stop by to spend time with Art and that she knew that a home health care nurse was set up to visit twice a week. She assured me that all was well and that she had it covered. Heather had also agreed to be there for Art and had been stopping by every couple days on her way to or from her job. So I settled into my life and my job and counted the days until I could go back to the Cape.

Art asked for very little, but last week he'd mentioned to me that he had a desire to have a bath. He must have mentioned it to Heather too. Since his apartment did not have a bathtub, Heather offered to take him to her place for a few days so that he could enjoy a bath there. I was so happy for him and grateful for Heather being in his life. Art had his bath and stayed for a few days at Heather's house, but he became restless and decided that he wanted to go back to his own apartment. I think he felt more comfortable at his place, or maybe did not want to be a burden to Heather or her boys.

When I arrived on Friday for my weekend visit, Art was sleeping in his recliner. I did not want to disturb him, so I quietly made myself at home. Something on his kitchen counter caught my eye. It was a new light blue plastic daily pill box with all his meds in order. I checked the pill bottles on the counter and noticed that there were several new prescriptions for anxiety and sleep. Then, I saw it; on the counter was a pamphlet from hospice...*Information for Family Members: Commonly Asked Questions About Dying.* My heart dropped to my toes. My first thoughts were, *Where did this come from? Do we really need this now? Is it time?* In my shock, I put two and two together and decided that the new home health care nurse was actually a hospice nurse. Dr. Brown must have decided it was time to help prepare Art and our family for what was ahead. I tried to calm myself by breathing deeply. I picked up the literature and took it to the balcony to look it over:

1. What occurs during the process of dying?
2. What are normal physical signs of dying?
3. What are some common mental and emotional changes seen when a person is dying?

Each point came with a list of possibilities that might or might not occur for every person. My eyes glazed over, and I could not read any more. This was becoming too real. Even though some part of me knew that Art's life was coming to an end, I just couldn't allow those thoughts in. Not now. Not yet.

When Art began to stir, I quickly hid the pamphlet, wiped my arm across my tear-stained face, and greeted him with a cheerful

"Guess who's here?"

"Hey, it's you! You're back! Come give me a hug," he said, looking up from his recliner.

"Who else were you expecting but one of your favorite admirers?" I laughed. "How has your week been?"

"Oh, just great," he said quietly. "Had a few visitors from the restaurant and a real cute nurse."

"Well, guess what? You have another visitor coming tomorrow."

"Who's that?" he replied.

"Randy."

"You mean Charlotte's son?"

"Yes, he's leading one of his Boy Scout trips to Europe soon and wanted to come visit with you before he left."

"That will be great, love to have him. By the way, I forget, is he the oldest?"

"No," I replied. "He's second. Remember, Scott is the oldest. Randy is a couple years older than my Jennifer. Let's see...that makes him maybe thirty-two? Do you remember that he is named after you?"

"That's right," he said with a big smile. "Randal Dean. I always forget my middle name is Dean. Wasn't I named after someone?"

"Yes, Arthur Dean, you were named after our father and his brother, Uncle Bob. You inherited both of their middle names: Charles Arthur and Robert Dean."

"Hmm, that's about all I got from them, but we won't go there."

I continued, "Randy is such a great guy and has been in Boy Scouts since he was a Cub Scout at six or seven years old. He's been a troop leader for many years and has helped so many boys become Eagle Scouts."

"One of these days I'd like to go on one of his trips," I said, kind of dreaming out loud. "Do you know that Charlotte is going on this trip?"

"Oh, so that's why she's going to Europe. Now I know he has his hands full!"

We both laughed.

Art settled in to watch a baseball game on the TV while I kept myself busy tidying up the place. Randy arrived on Saturday to spend some time with Uncle Art. He pulled up a chair and they watched baseball together. I could hear that Art was having a hard time following the game, a game which he not only played but knew inside and out.

"Isn't it the last inning?" he asked.

"No, they're just finishing the seventh," offered Randy.

"But didn't he bat in the last inning? I guess I must have dozed off," Art said with a confused look.

Randy and I exchanged puzzled glances and kept the conversation going. Out of nowhere, Art sat up, pushed his recliner to a more seated position, and said, "I have an idea. Let's go to the grocery store. I have a few things to pick up."

Randy and I locked eyes again and hunched our shoulders as if to say, *What do you think?* And I said, "Sure, let's go."

We had no idea how this little venture would go because lately, Art had only been out of his apartment to go to his doctor's office, but we agreed that we were up for it.

Art allowed Randy to hold his arm and help him down the stairs. "Watch your step, Uncle Art. It's a big one," Randy said as he helped him up into the passenger seat of his new green Jeep.

"Whoa, this is a beauty. Now we're riding in style," Art said to Randy, giving him a thumbs-up.

I jumped in the back seat and we were off, driving along the back roads of Hyannis. Randy put all the windows down and Art seemed to enjoy just being out. I could see the beach and water between the houses, and the smell of the salt water in the air was heavenly. All of a sudden, Art said, "Hey, that's where Heather works. Let's stop by for a quick one."

So, happy to do anything for Uncle Art, Randy said, "Sure," and pulled into a parking space right in front of Kerrigan's Restaurant. As luck would have it, Heather was working at the bar and was surprised and delighted to see us. She said, "Hey, look who's here. So good to see all of you."

Art said, "You remember my nephew Randy? You know he is named after me," he boasted as if he was proud to have a namesake.

"Well, you know what I'll have," Art joked. Heather reached for his favorite Captain Morgan and Coke.

I hesitated and then said, "Art, are you sure you can drink that along with your new meds?"

He laughed and said, "It's only a weak one; she knows what I like."

Oh well, I thought to myself. *At this point, would it really matter?*

After a drink and a short visit, we said our goodbyes and proceeded on to the grocery store. Randy parked as close as he could, but when we got out of the Jeep, I realized that it was still a bit of a walk to the store entrance. I noticed that Art was walking very tentatively, gathering his balance between steps. When we got inside the store, I quickly pulled over a shopping cart and said, "Here you go, Mr. Westfall; it's your trip, so you get to push the cart," hoping this would help to steady him.

"So what is it you were wanting?" I asked as we slowly wandered the aisles.

He looked unsure and puzzled, as though he did not know where he was or maybe even why we were there. Randy and I shot each other another look. I said, "Well, let's pick up some burgers for supper—how will that be for tonight?" We all agreed that it would be a good choice. Randy and I quickly found what we would need for dinner. "My treat," I said as we checked out.

"Ahh, you don't have to do that, you're my guests," Art said, attempting to pay.

"No way," I insisted. "How often do I get to treat two good-looking guys to dinner?"

We made our way out of the store with Art pushing the cart. Once again, my heart felt like it was breaking…this was becoming a familiar feeling.

The next day we hung out, watching baseball again and just being there with Art as he dozed off and on in his recliner. It was a beautiful day, and I had an idea. Since Randy was still there, and there were now two of us to help, I said, full of excitement, "Hey, how about the three of us go on the Cat Boat?"

"What's that?" Randy asked.

"It's a beautiful sailboat that goes out of the harbor just down the street," I enthusiastically answered.

Art sleepily said, "No, I can't do that today."

"Aw, come on, Art, we'll all go! It'll be fun!" I pleaded.

"Nah, not for me today. Randy, come over here."

I heard him as he whispered in Randy's ear, "Go over to that bureau and get some money out of my sock in the corner of the top drawer. Take your aunt on the Cat Boat."

"No, no, we don't want to go without you," I said.

"I'll be fine. I'll just take a nap. I really, really want you to do this," he said.

And so we did. Randy and I walked down to the harbor and bought our tickets with Art's sock money. I had my adventure on the Cat Boat with the wind blowing through my hair and the tears running down my cheeks.

CHAPTER SIXTEEN

The weekend after Randy came to visit and said what was to be his final goodbye to Uncle Art, I decided to stay at Art's apartment until Eileen could get there to relieve me. I called her and explained that I thought it was time that we not leave Art alone if we could avoid it. Although Art never complained about anything but his "damn big toe," he just wasn't himself. Lately he seemed somewhat confused, and I wondered if it was caused by his intermittent sleep. Eileen agreed and offered to come to the Cape on Sunday night so that we could spend a little time together and I could hand off our patient so that neither of us would worry so much.

Monday morning, I was getting ready to leave for home and feeling better about leaving Art with Eileen. He woke up in his recliner, where he now slept all the time. He looked at me and said, "I think I want to go into the office today to get the ordering done."

Except for our grocery store adventure with Randy, Art had not been out of his apartment in the past three weeks. Eileen and I looked at each other with a wide-eyed look as if to say, *Now what do we do?* By now, I assumed Pufferbellies had replaced Art, but I didn't have the heart to tell him. I hesitated, waiting for an answer to come, and finally I said, "You sure you want to do that?"

"Hell yes," he replied. "Got to get supplies in for the weekend. I don't want to let them down."

I thought for another moment and then to my surprise I said, "You know, Art, if I was your mother, I probably would not do this, but since you don't ask for anything and we're two of your favorite sisters, let's do it!"

Like three little kids excited to go to a birthday party, we got ready to go. As Art got up from his chair, he fell right on his butt and lay there laughing. He looked up at Eileen, and with a wink and a confused smile, he said to her, "Are you having fun yet?"

We got him up from the floor and helped him walk toward the bathroom.

"I've got this, I've got this," he said, pushing us away and walking on his own.

When he came back out, he looked at us and said, "OK, find me something to wear."

We picked out one of his favorite outfits and helped him get dressed. Hawaiian shirt, khaki shorts, and of course his best leather flip-flops. He was ready to go as if it were any other workday. But were we ready? My mind raced as I thought of what the staff at Pufferbellies would say or do when we got there. Would they understand why we brought him there? Would they be shocked at his weight loss? Would they play the game with us?

As we went to get into Art's car, Eileen and I again looked at each other with fear in our eyes. What were we going to do? We both knew that he shouldn't be driving anymore.

Eileen quickly said, "Hey, Art, how about letting me drive your convertible, like old times?"

Thank God he easily agreed. Whew! Dodged that bullet. Eileen quickly got in the driver's seat with Art riding shotgun. I took the chaperone spot in the back seat. As we backed out of the driveway, I found myself remembering when Art had owned a big boat of a powder-blue Chevy convertible in the sixties. That was when he and Eileen were both in high school. So the story goes, Art, the younger of the two, had somehow bought a car. After a short period of time, he decided that he couldn't afford to keep it and sold it to Eileen. I almost laughed out loud when I remembered he sold the car to Eileen because he had a new steady girlfriend who had a car. The new girlfriend drove him around so that he didn't need the cost of a car or the insurance. I smiled when I recalled that they were only thirteen months apart and had really enjoyed growing up together. Recently in looking through Art's papers, I found the handwritten bill of sale for that car, which read:

> I agree to give my sister my car for $200 and she is to take over the payments of $66.20 a month. I will get $100 cash and the rest when she can give it to me.
> Signed:
> Arthur Dean Westfall
> Eileen Westfall
> Augustine W. Cuomo
> Margaret Cuomo

With the top down on Art's convertible and our shades on, we set off for our morning adventure to Pufferbellies. I looked at my watch and realized it was only 8:30 a.m. I had another thought: *Would anyone be at Pufferbellies?* Since it was a nightclub and closed at one or two in the morning, most of the staff didn't arrive for setup until at least noon. Oh well, I guess we'd find out...we were on our way.

Since Art lived only ten minutes from Pufferbellies, we were there in no time. As predicted, there were only a couple cars in the parking lot. The three of us stepped out of the car and headed to the side door. Fortunately, the door was ajar, as I don't think Art had remembered to bring his keys. We walked in and adjusted our eyes from the sunlight. I saw Art's boss, John Morgan, and several other people working behind the bar. I held my breath. "Hey, guys, how's it going? I thought I would come get the supply orders in," Art said cheerfully.

John looked up and squinted his eyes in disbelief, as if he was looking at a ghost. "Well, hey, Art...uh, good to see you," he politely replied as he tried to keep his composure. "What are you doing here?"

Art replied as though it was a normal day, "Oh, just thought I would check in, do the orders, and make sure everything was going OK."

One of the other guys stepped in to greet Art. "Hey, buddy, how's it going?"

"OK, you know, fair to middling," Art chuckled. "You all know my sisters, right?"

"Yeah, sure, Art," John managed to say. "How are you girls doing?"

It began to get awkward; no one knew what to say, least of all me. So I hesitantly replied, "Oh, we're great, John. Just visiting the Cape to keep this guy in line."

Art looked around the bar and said, "Well, I'll just take a look in the storeroom to see what we need for the weekend."

As Art slowly walked toward the storage area, John looked at me wide-eyed, as if to say, *What do we do?* I closed my eyes, squeezed in the tears, and scrunched my shoulders up to my ears as if to say, *I don't know, what do we do?* Shortly, Art came walking back with a disappointed look on his face and said, "I guess you're all set. Looks like you don't need anything."

We all seemed to be holding our breath and silently trying to figure out what to say or do next. John, who had been looking at the floor, raised his eyes and said, "Yes, Art, we're all set. We knew you were not able to come in on a regular basis, so Tony has taken over the ordering. You just take care of yourself, and we won't be needing you to come in anymore. I'll drop your checks in the mail."

Art had a look of confusion and disbelief as he calmly replied, "Well, OK, I guess I'll be seeing you guys."

He turned and began to shuffle his feet toward the door.

Eileen and I said our goodbyes and when John gave me a hug, he whispered in my ear, "I am so sorry."

I replied, "I know. Me too."

Eileen and I picked up what dignity Art had left and followed him out the door. *Don't cry, don't cry,* I pleaded with myself, not even able to look at Eileen, who is so much better at stuffing her feelings than I am. As we drove out of the Pufferbellies parking lot, Art adjusted his baseball cap and pulled the bill down to cover his eyes. He too was fighting back tears. Still stunned, none of us said a word as we drove through the center of Hyannis. Finally after what seemed like hours, Art said, with his usual boyhood glee, "I have an idea; let me buy you girls an ice cream!"

An ice cream was the furthest thing from my mind, as it was now only nine o'clock in the morning. But what did I say? "Sure, Art. Great idea. Let's do it."

Eileen raised her eyebrows and gave me a look of disbelief as she found a place to park. The three of us got out of the car and walked arm in arm like the Lion, Scarecrow, and Tin Man from *The Wizard of Oz.* We went straight to Ben and Jerry's and ordered ice cream cones. Yes—at nine o'clock in the morning, we ate ice cream.

CHAPTER SEVENTEEN

After Art's visit to Pufferbellies, where he found out that his job had been replaced, he became very quiet and did not engage in conversation as much. He seemed content to settle into his recliner and nap off and on. I noticed it had become harder for him to concentrate on reading the newspaper, and even TV programs held little interest. He would often start reading, and the next time I looked at him, the newspaper would be in his lap and he would be dozing.

One of the highlights of his day—and mine—was reading the heartfelt cards that his friends and patrons from Pufferbellies sent to him. They wished him well, mentioned they were praying for him, and expressed how much they missed him. Several said how Pufferbellies was not the same without him. He got such a kick out of the cards that shared a personal joke or a special memory. One of the cards especially touched my heart. It read:

Dear Artie,

How can we ever thank you enough for all that you have done for us? You have become such a treasured friend. You have shared in our happiness right from the very beginning, and you've been there for us every step of the way. From our first dates at Pufferbellies, to our New Year's Eve engagement, our Jack and Jill, and our wedding party at Pufferbellies. You've given us so much—the best wedding party, complete with a champagne toast.

But most special to us is the wonderful friendship we share with you. Thank you, Artie. You are one special person and we are so gifted because of your friendship and your truly caring ways. We thank you for all you've done for us.

We love you.
Al and Linda

Now that it seemed Art was in more pain and discomfort, I was so thankful that the home health nurse continued to visit every other day. She suggested that Art have a PICC line inserted in his arm with a PCA pump, which would allow him to push a button to release more medication to control the pain as needed. Dr. Brown agreed. Not only did the meds control the pain, but they seemed to relax Art, relieve his anxiety, and allow him to sleep more comfortably.

Eileen and her husband, Lou, decided to give me a break and cover the next weekend with Art. While it was not easy for me to stay away, I agreed. Eileen called me several times over that weekend and expressed her concern that Art was failing quickly. She shared that Lou had helped Art shower and shave. Lou had even gone as far as to get in the shower stall with Art. She told me that he and Art had a good laugh over that one. Before Lou left to go home, he wrote this on a lined pad:

Sunday night, August 11, 1996
Art seems to be lapsing into dazed silence more often. His intelligence, when alert, seems in good order. He realizes that Eileen is here, that Lou is here. When he "comes back," he seems to be confused and scared.

I think he is not in "cancer pain" but is feeling the effects of his nonmovement.

Art's conscious self is telling him he is dying; the medicated Art is creating confusion and anxiety. The back and forth, in and out is causing frustration. Art, when alert, is breaking down, and thanks to Eileen, is finding some comfort. Thankfully he seems to return to the dazed state quite rapidly. If not called or moved, he seems content to be there.

P.S.: I hope if hospice finds room for him that he will find someone there who will help him in and out of these states. I know God will be with him during this time and soon he will be reunited with his mother.

We pray for him and that we have the strength to help him on his journey. If this suffering leads to eternal happiness, then I find happiness in my heart for him.

On Monday morning, just as I arrived at my office, I got a call from Eileen from the Cape. She was crying and distraught. She said through her tears, "You have to come. I can't do this by myself."

I gulped and said, "Let me put things together here and I'll be on my way."

I went to my boss and told him I had to leave for the Cape. He said, "Go, our hearts go with you; just keep us posted."

"Thanks," was all that I could say.

He and my coworkers had been so understanding throughout this whole process. I drove home not able to think. I went on autopilot and quickly packed a bag. There was no time to make meals for this trip. I was thankful that I knew the route by heart, but I seemed to be driving in slow motion. I needed to get there. Eileen would not have called if she didn't think it was necessary. "I can't do this by myself" rang in my ears.

Finally I arrived at Art's apartment. Eileen, who had been watching out the upstairs window, met me at the downstairs door. "I've called hospice; it's time," she said. "We can't do this here anymore."

Still in denial and disbelief, I nodded my head. "What did they say?" I asked.

"They're going to find a bed for him at the hospice house in Barnstable as quickly as possible. Hopefully this afternoon," she replied.

I took a deep breath and said, "Remember: we're doing this together."

We hugged and started up the stairs to Art's apartment. Eileen grabbed my arm, pulled me back, and said, "I told Art that you were coming and he said, 'She's having a real hard time with this.'"

Now I couldn't hold back the tears, so we held each other and cried.

After sharing all the tissues we had between us, I said, "OK, OK, we can do this. Let's go up."

Art was sitting on the couch in a semi-reclining position with his head back, kind of dozing. I went and sat beside him and quietly said, "Hey, guy, I'm here."

He gave me a hug and remarked with a grin, "It's about time."

I hesitated as I took a big inhale and said, "Yes, it's time. We're trying to get a room for you at the hospice house in Barnstable. They hope to have one today. You will be so much more comfortable there."

"You think so?" he replied. "OK, then let's go." And he tried to stand up.

"Well, Art, we have to wait until we get the call letting us know that they have a room," offered Eileen.

Again, he insisted, "Let's go," as if he was ready.

So Eileen and I helped him up and decided to walk him around the room to kill some time. We had no idea how hard this would be. He put an arm around each of our shoulders and we attempted to walk with him. At one point he stopped, looked over at Eileen, who was on his right, tapped his cheek with his finger, and she immediately gave him a kiss on the cheek. He then turned his head in my direction and tapped his left cheek. I, too, gave him a kiss on the cheek. He gazed at me with a faraway look and quietly said, "I owe you."

I replied just as quietly with a slight grin, "You're damned right you do. You better be there for us when it's our turn."

He nodded as though he understood. As we continued to walk with him around his apartment, he became more anxious and agitated and seemed to be in some pain. I am not sure he understood where we were going, but he was ready to go and wanted to go right then. The phone rang, startling all of us. Was this the bittersweet call we were all waiting for? Eileen stepped away to answer it and I managed to get Art into his recliner. "Yes," she replied. "This is his sister. What time? OK, we will be there. Yes, we'll bring everything."

She put the phone down and nodded to me. "They have a room."

Art had dozed off again in his chair, so he did not notice that we were hugging and crying again.

"Oh my God, this is it," I mumbled through my tears.

"They told me we can come anytime after two," she said. "We need to bring his meds and personal items."

Trying to wrap my mind around it, I said, "OK, OK, we can do this. How about I gather the meds and paperwork and you get some clothes and personal items together?"

"What will I put his stuff in?" asked Eileen. "Does he have a suitcase?"

"No, no, just use that wicker laundry basket in the corner. It will work," I replied, as if it was a sense of urgency and we had to hurry.

Art aroused just about the time we had everything put together that we thought he might need. He was confused, so we waited a few minutes for him to be more awake and alert. I said as gently as I could, "Art, they have a room for you at the hospice, so we're going to go now."

"Good, let's go," he said, as if we were off to a special event.

I'm not sure he really understood where we were going, but he was ready.

Just then Eileen said, "Oh no, it's pouring outside."

"I'll go down and ask Alice if she will open the garage door, and I will pull up inside so we can get him into my car," I said with a nod.

I ran downstairs and told Alice what was going on and asked her for help with the garage door.

She immediately replied, "Of course I will open the door. Oh, my dear…I am so glad that you both are here. You'll keep me posted, won't you?"

"Yes. I will for sure," I said.

As I went to run back up the stairs, I turned back and said in a panic, "Oh, wait a minute. I don't know how to get there."

Alice quickly got a used envelope from her desk and wrote down the directions for me. This was long before Google Maps or cell phones.

I went back upstairs and said to Eileen, "How the heck are we going to get him down the stairs?"

Now Eileen took the lead and said, "Come on, we have to do it."

Art cooperated the best he could. It was a good thing he was already dressed. We helped him put on his favorite Pufferbellies windbreaker and his faded Kahlua baseball cap. "Ready?" I asked.

He looked at me sadly for a moment and then with that twinkle in his eye said, "Ready."

Even though it was such a special place to him, I believe Art did not want to die in his apartment. Nor do I believe he wanted us to handle this by ourselves. He knew it was time, and he faced it with the same courage and selflessness he'd dealt with his fate the entire time.

We helped him to the top of the stairs and prepared to go down. It almost seemed as if he had forgotten how to walk or that he didn't know what to do to make his legs work. So I said, "Art, let's do this one step down at a time. Here we go; on three. One...two...three...step." And that's how we got him down the stairs, one step at a time.

My car was running at the edge of the open garage. Somehow, we managed to get Art in the front seat and Eileen and the laundry basket in the back seat. I buckled him in and then I buckled myself. As I pushed in the clutch and put my car in gear, Art looked over at me and said, "Marylin, you can't drive this car."

I looked back over at him and replied, "Of course I can, Art, it's my car. I've been driving a stick for a while now. You'll see."

He grinned and said, "OK, if you say so." Then he settled back into his seat like an obedient little boy.

Alice waved to us from the open garage door. Our eyes locked for a moment. I think we both knew Art would not be coming back to his sweet little waterview apartment.

CHAPTER EIGHTEEN

I t was pouring so hard I could hardly see to drive. With Alice's handwritten directions in one hand and my windshield wipers on high, I headed toward the hospice house in Barnstable. I quickly realized I couldn't drive and read at the same time, so I reached back and handed the directions to Eileen in the back seat so she could read them to me.

I drove slowly along Ocean Street, being careful of the people in their rain gear crossing the street to board the island ferries. I crossed over Main Street and could see a lot of traffic up ahead.

"Oh no," I said. "Look at all the traffic. I think every vacationer is out on the road today, and all the tour buses too."

Art perked up and said with his usual grin, "Yep, all the blue-heads and almost-deads headed out to fill up the restaurants for lunch. You girls hungry?" It seemed he had forgotten where we were going.

"No, Art. We're not hungry," piped up Eileen. "We'll get something later." She then asked, "Art, do you know another way to Barnstable?"

He looked out the rain-soaked windows and appeared confused. "I'll tell you later," he said, as if he just couldn't figure it out.

I looked at Eileen in the rearview mirror and we both knew there would not be a later. The windows began to fog up, so I turned on the defroster and used the back of my hand to wipe the windshield so I could see. From the back seat, Eileen warned me, "Get ready; there's a rotary coming up and you'll need to get off at the second exit." Sure enough, there it was right up ahead of me. "Oh no, I hate these," I said in desperation. "Who ever thought these up anyway? Hold on, here we go."

Clutching the steering wheel tightly, around the rotary I went and managed to get off at the second exit onto Route 132, Iyannough Road. "Woohoo!" I shouted and pumped my fist. "Did it on my first time around!"

The traffic continued bumper-to-bumper as we passed the IHOP on the right. Cars were pulling in and out of restaurants and shopping plazas. I kept telling myself, *Breathe, be calm, you can do this.*

"There! Look up ahead," said Eileen.

I saw a big green-and-white sign that read: Barnstable Village, next right. I took a deep breath and finally felt confident that we were going in the right direction. With the rain still coming down in buckets and the windshield wipers trying to keep up, we all settled in for the rest of the ride. Besides the flap-flap noise of the wipers trying to keep up with the rain, it was silent in the car. Art dozed in the front seat while Eileen stared out the side window from the back seat. I was quiet too. None of us knew what lay ahead of us.

We turned right onto Hyannis-Barnstable Road and continued to follow the signs to Barnstable Village. After about thirty minutes, which seemed like hours, we arrived at Main Street. At Eileen's direction, I took a left and saw a railroad crossing up ahead and remembered Alice had said it was near the tracks and quite close to a prison. "I think this is it. Railroad Avenue," I said. I drove tentatively down the street, looking at the houses on either side. I pointed to a big house at the dead end of the street and said, "Is that it? Eileen, can you read the sign?" Leaning over the front seat to get a better look, she said, "Yes, that's it. Barnstable Hospice House." It was just as I had pictured it: a homey-looking two-story oversized Colonial-style house with weather-stained gray shingles and white shutters. Just then, there was a loud clap of thunder, startling all of us. The sky opened up, and it was raining even harder. I pulled up as close as I could to the front door. I said to Eileen, "OK, this is it. Now we just have to get him inside." I gently nudged Art. "OK, Art, we're here," I said softly, as though we had just arrived at some special destination.

"I'm ready. But Jesus, you might have to help me out of this contraption," he said as he struggled with his seat belt.

I reached over and unbuckled him. The rain continued to come down in what felt like a waterfall. Eileen and I both jumped out of the car to help him, as if there was a reason to hurry. The three of us managed to walk the short distance together, arm in arm, the same way we had gotten him out of the house—one… two…three…step. I rang the doorbell but didn't wait for anyone to answer. I just turned the knob and pushed open the front door of the house, and we all shoved our way in. We must have been quite the sight. All three of us were soaked from the rain—dripping hair, T-shirts clinging to us, and wet feet in our flip-flops. Eileen and I were on either side of Art, steadying him the best we could. Straight ahead at the end of a narrow hallway, I saw two nurses in blue scrubs. They immediately came to greet us. "Ah, you must be Art. We have been expecting you," said the cute little blond nurse.

"That's me," Art said sheepishly, looking up from under the bill of his baseball cap. "And these are my sisters."

The other nurse stepped forward with a look of disbelief. We must have been quite a sight, the three of us soaking wet and Eileen and I with a shoulder under each of Art's arms, helping him to stand. Both nurses glanced at each other, and I imagined them thinking to themselves, *How on earth did you get him here on your own today, and how have you been able to keep him at home?* To this day, this is something I had never thought about. Art was our brother, and we did what we thought was best for him. Bringing him to the hospice any sooner or calling an ambulance had never entered our minds.

"I'm Nancy," said the young blond one. "This is Mary. We have a nice private room for you, so let's get you dried off and settled in. All right, Art?"

"OK, babe, whatever you say," replied Art shyly with his signature grin and a wink.

Mary said, "Let's get you ladies a couple of towels so you can dry off, and then you can make yourselves comfortable in the living room across the hall. We'll call you in when we have Art settled."

Reluctantly, we turned Art over to the nurses. The two of them stepped forward to steady Art. We watched as they helped him walk down the hall, arm in arm. It felt as though they had replaced us. Before we attempted to dry ourselves off, Eileen and I headed back outside so I could move my car and we could bring Art's belongings in.

It was then I realized the wicker basket was overflowing with Art's clothes. I smiled to myself and thought, *I wonder what Eileen was thinking? Will he really need all these clothes? Oh well,* I said to myself. *I guess we won't need to do any of Art's laundry for a while.* When we came back inside, shivering from our wet clothes, we found the living room, which was warm and cozy. It was furnished with some outdated colonial maple furniture, including a couple sofas, two floor lamps, and a faded orange -and-brown-oval-hooked rug. We each found a seat and tried to dry off with the towels. I tried to settle down and began looking for something to read. I noticed several piles of what appeared to be scrapbooks on the coffee table. I picked one up and turned a few pages before I quickly realized what they were: remembrance books. Each page was uniquely laid out. The one common item was a clear plastic page holder with a newspaper obituary and a spray of pressed dried flowers. I held my breath when I realized that these were all people who had passed away here at the Barnstable Hospice House. I snapped the book closed and once again fought back tears, thinking, *Oh my God, is Art really going to die and have a page in one of these books?* I couldn't bear to show it to

Eileen, not now…not yet.

Just then, Nancy came to the doorway and said, "OK, Art's all set. Do you ladies want to come in and join him?"

Eileen picked up the wicker basket and we followed the nurse down the hall to his room. It was a very plain yet welcoming corner room. Straight ahead was a window with blue-and-purple hydrangea-printed curtains, looking very "Cape Cod." There were two folding chairs—one by the bedside and the other in the corner. On the wall across from the end of Art's bed was a sliding door that appeared to open to a garden area. To our surprise, Art was sitting up in a hospital bed wearing a light blue johnny coat and was relatively alert. He seemed calm and content to be there.

Nancy said, "OK, Art, now that you're settled in, would you like something to eat? What's your favorite sandwich?"

Although he had not been eating much of anything, Art replied, "A BLT, of course."

"No problem, one BLT coming right up. That we can do." And out the door she went.

Eileen and I shot each other a look and shrugged our shoulders. I wondered if we should have told her that he probably wouldn't eat anything. But I guess she would find out. As soon as the nurse left the room, Art began to doze again, but when she came back with his sandwich, he perked up and said, "Thanks, babe." Then he picked up the sandwich and took a small bite.

"OK," she said cheerfully, enjoy," and left the room.

After a few minutes, Eileen, who was watching Art like a mother hen, realized he was still chewing the same bite and trying to sleep at the same time. She reached over, held out her hand, and said, "Art, do you want me to take the rest of that?" He looked confused but seemed relieved to spit the rest of the bacon into the napkin that she was holding.

"Art, why don't you just sit back and rest, and we'll be right here," I said.

"Promise?" he said.

"Yes, of course. We're not going anywhere. We'll be right here if you need us."

"OK, that would be great," he uttered as he closed his eyes.

Eileen and I pulled up the chairs and settled in by his bedside. It was not long before he woke up with a startled look on his face, as if he didn't know where he was. We once again assured him that we were there and he settled down, but shortly began to moan as though he was in some pain. A nurse's aide walking by must have heard him, as she immediately came in. I said, "He seems to be in some pain. Anything that can be done?" I pointed and continued, "He has a PCA pump right here in his arm."

She looked at me and said, "Honey, he can't do it himself any-more, but..." She looked around the room as if to see if anyone was listening. Her eyes went from me to the PCA pump and back a couple times. I finally got it. "Oh, you mean I can do it?" She raised her eyebrows and hunched her shoulders as if to say, *You're the one sitting there, and he can't do it himself.* I looked at Eileen and knew she had gotten the message too. *OK,* I said to myself. *Game on.* I figured out how to push the button and make the pump work. If pumping medication into his arm was going to help keep the pain level down, I would do it. I was thankful that after a short while, nurse Nancy came in and told us they would give him something to help him sleep through the night.

She assured us that a doctor would visit Art the next day and help determine what he needed to keep him comfortable. Eileen and I stayed by Art's bedside, comforting him the best we could. We continued to assure him that we were there until he was sleeping soundly as a baby. By that time, we were both falling asleep in our chairs. The night nurse encouraged us to go home to get a good night's sleep and come back the next day. We reluctantly agreed and found our way back to Art's apartment in Hyannis.

CHAPTER NINETEEN

Eileen and I woke up the next morning at Art's apartment. "How did you sleep?" I asked.

"Not much," she answered. "You?"

"Not much either," I replied.

We were both unusually quiet as we took turns getting showered and dressed for the day. We seemed to be deep in our own thoughts, or at a loss for words. I'm not sure which. "Are you almost ready?" I said. "Do you think we forgot to take anything yesterday?"

"No," she responded. "I think we're good."

"OK, then let's go."

As we were heading to the car, Alice poked her head out of her door and said, "How's it going? Did you get Art settled in OK?"

"Yes. We're headed back to the hospice now," I replied.

"OK. Just know our thoughts and prayers go with you. Art is a special guy to us."

"Thanks," I replied. "And thanks for all you have done for Art and us. We'll keep you posted."

We headed back to Barnstable. The sun was shining and there was very little traffic. This time, I even managed to navigate the rotaries without swearing. When we arrived at the hospice, I was glad to see that the same nurses were on duty: Nancy (Art's "babe") and Mary. Nancy greeted us and said, "Art had a pretty good night, but he is now experiencing some pain. The on-call doctor is scheduled to stop by to see him soon."

We walked down the narrow hall to his room. As we entered, I could hear Art moaning.

"We're here, buddy," I said.

"Oh, good. About time," he replied, hardly opening his eyes.

For the next couple of hours, Eileen and I took turns sitting by his bedside, holding his hand and assuring him that we were there. At one point, he motioned me closer and quietly said, "There's some checks in my top drawer. I want you to go cash them."

"OK," I said. "I can do that."

For some reason, I got the impression that he wanted me to do it *now*. So I asked Eileen, "Can you hold the fort while I go to Hyannis? I'll be back as soon as I can."

"Sure," she agreed. "You go do what you have to do and I'll be right here."

I didn't know how I was going to be able to accomplish this. But I was going to go back to his apartment, get those checks, and do as Art asked. As I went to leave the room, I noticed Art's windbreaker hanging on a hook by the door. I don't know what made me do it, but I reached in the pocket, found his wallet, and took his driver's license. I thought, *Maybe it will help*. I left the hospice and made my way back to Art's apartment in Hyannis. Sure enough, in his sock drawer, stashed in an old white tube sock, there were several paychecks from Pufferbellies. I signed Art's name on the back of each check and my name right below. I drove to his bank nearby in Hyannis Center, praying all the way that this would work. I drove up to the drive-thru window and took a deep breath. A pretty thirty-something young woman greeted me as she pushed the metal drawer my way. I put the checks and both Art's driver's license and mine in the tray. When she took them out, she looked up at me with a smile and said, "How's Art doing?"

Stunned that she knew him, I answered, "Oh, OK, I guess. You know...one day at a time...uh...I'm his sister," I stammered as confidently as I could, hoping that it would make me credible. I did not tell her that Art was in the hospice in Barnstable. I just couldn't. She proceeded to prepare the cash from the checks as normal. When she pushed the drawer back out to me, she said, "Please tell Art that Laurie at the bank was asking about him." And with a business-as-usual look on her face and a twinkle in her eye, she said, "Have a nice day."

I thanked her, put my car in gear, and drove out of the bank lot. My heart was racing. Even though I felt like I had just robbed a bank in broad daylight, I knew it was the right thing to do for Art. I drove the now-familiar route back to the hospice in Barnstable. When I arrived, Eileen, looking as white as a ghost, greeted me at the door of Art's room. "We have to talk," she immediately said, motioning to the hallway.

"OK, what's up?" I asked.

"Let's go outside," she said.

We found our way along a brick path to a garden area in the back of the building and sat on a park bench. She grabbed me, hugged me, and burst into tears. "The doctor was here," she said, sobbing. "And they want to start giving him morphine. You know what that means. I told them that they couldn't do that, at least not until you got back. I said, 'My sister needs to be here before you begin. And she needs to agree.'"

Now I was sobbing. I didn't know what to think, what to do. I knew exactly why she had made them wait. A vivid memory flashed before my eyes. Only a little more than a year ago, our mother had been admitted to a hospice in Connecticut. The nurses told us that they were going to keep her comfortable and ease her pain by giving her morphine. We assumed this was best for her even though she had not been complaining of pain and had been able to communicate with us up until that point. To our surprise, after they started the morphine, we never had a conversation with her again. I am sure it was the right thing for her at the time, but I don't think that we really realized that was going to be the end. She passed away peacefully a couple of days later.

I felt panic setting in. What should we do? Should we let them start giving him morphine? "Let's go back to Art's room and see how he's doing," I said. "Maybe he will help us make this decision."

We went back to Art's room and found that he was writhing in pain and becoming more anxious, agitated, and not really alert. His favorite nurse, Nancy, came into the room and asked if she could talk with us. We followed her to the living room. Since there was no one else in the room, she was able to talk freely. She began by saying, "I know this is not easy to hear, but Art is in the last stages of life and nothing more can be done for him except to keep him comfortable and as pain-free as possible." She also said, "The doctor ordered the medication to do that. What do you want to do? Are you ready for us to begin administering the meds?"

My mind raced. Denial was beginning to crumble. On some level, I knew Art was dying, but I just couldn't let it in. *Is this really happening?* We had only brought Art here yesterday. Yet in my heart of hearts, I knew it was time. I didn't want Art to suffer in pain. I knew what we had to do. We had been here for him all the way and we couldn't stop advocating for him now. We would certainly do what was best for Art.

Eileen and I looked at each other, unable to say a word. We nodded our heads, yes.

"OK," I said. "But before you begin, let us have a few minutes to talk with him."

"Yes, of course, take your time," acknowledged Nancy, who was beside us with a comforting hand on my shoulder. "You let us know when you're ready. We'd also like you to choose something for him to wear."

With blurry eyes, we started toward his room. Were they asking us to choose something for Art to wear to die in? We also knew the answer to that one. We made our way back to Art's room, one foot in front of the other. Art seemed to be settling down as the nurses were bathing him and changing his sheets. We found our wicker basket filled with his clothes in the corner of his room and began to aimlessly look through it. I picked up a few shirts and put them back. "How about this light blue button-down with 'Pufferbellies' embroidered on it?" said Eileen, holding up a long-sleeved Oxford shirt.

"No, that's too much like work," I muttered.

We each held up a few more shirts, continuing to reject them, as they were just not right. When I picked up the next shirt, I knew it was "the one."

"This one, this one!" I exclaimed. "This is one from his happy, fun days."

It was a light heather-gray T-shirt with a navy-blue silhouette of a surfer riding the crest of a wave across the words "Wellfleet." I remembered him saying how much he had liked to fish and surf with Heather's sons along the Wellfleet beaches. I think it was off this shore that he caught a small shark. He told such hilarious stories about how he had put it in the trunk of his car and it thumped all the way home. He decided to take it back and release it. Spending time with those boys were some of his happiest days. Eileen and I agreed; that shirt would be the one. While we were in the corner of his room choosing the perfect shirt, the nurse began the medication. Making this decision was one of the hardest things we had done. We hoped and prayed we had made the best choice for Art. Eileen and I slowly made our way to his bedside. From either side of his bed, we each held one of his hands as we kissed him on the cheek and assured him that we were going to be there with him.

I handed the chosen T-shirt to nurse Nancy, and we stepped out to begin our wait in the living room while they finished dressing him.

CHAPTER TWENTY

When we went back into his room, Art was wearing the T-shirt we had chosen. He already seemed calmer and somewhat at peace. "We're here, Art; we're going to be right here," I quietly offered, as if to not disturb him.

We pulled up two folding chairs to his bedside, and Eileen and I prepared to wait. Wait for what, we were not sure. By now it was early evening. We were getting hungry and thought about going out for a quick bite to eat. The nursing shifts were about to switch over to the evening crew. As they were leaving, nurses Nancy and Mary came to say their goodbyes to us.

"OK," Eileen said. "Thanks, and we'll see you tomorrow."

"We appreciate all you've done for Art today," I said. "See you in the morning."

The two nurses looked at each other as though they knew something we didn't. Mary hesitated for a moment and then said, "Yeah, sure...see you tomorrow."

It was not long before a new evening nurse came into Art's room.

"Hi, I'm Ruth," she said. "I'm the head nurse on tonight's shift."

"Oh, nice to meet you," I said. "We were just about to go out for a quick bite to eat."

"Can we talk in the hallway for a minute before you leave?" she asked.

We followed her out to the nurses' station. When I looked at her again, I noticed she looked anxious and had tears in her eyes. She gathered her composure and in a shaky voice said, "This is my first night on as the head nurse here at the hospice, and they tell me your brother might not make it overnight. I hope I can handle it."

I was stunned at what I had just heard. My first thought was, *If you're not going to be able to handle it, how the heck will we be able to handle it?* She began to gently cry and apologize through her tears. Out of the corner of my eye, I saw the nurse's aide that had been in and out of Art's room all day. She was standing quietly in the hallway. She was the same one that had helped encourage me to use the PCA pump. This time, I noticed that she had soft blue eyes, just like our mother's. I turned to look at her again, and she shook her head and silently mouthed, "No. Don't go… stay. He needs you."

That's all I needed. If this head nurse was not confident in what to do, I was determined that we were going to be here for Art no matter what.

I said to Eileen, loud enough for everyone to hear, "OK, then, we are going to stay."

Ruth, the head nurse, seemed relieved and offered to have the kitchen make us something to eat. We decided to take a walk to the living room to try and make sense of what had just happened.

I said to Eileen, "Well…we don't know what to do either, but we can't leave Art here with her. It looks like we are here for the night."

"That's for damned sure," she said. "We're not leaving him with her."

And so our night began.

Word must have gotten out among Art's friends that he was at the hospice. We received several calls from people wanting to know if they could come to visit. We told them his situation and suggested that they not come that evening, as Art was now pretty calm and not really able to communicate. The only person who would not take "no" for an answer was his good friend, Linda. "Please, I want to be there," she gently insisted. "Could I please come?" Eileen and I relented, and I said, "OK, come." When I look back, I am so glad that she did.

Linda arrived at about ten o'clock and we continued our bedside vigil. Art was mostly calm and appeared to be resting or sleeping. The three of us stood together around his bed. "You know," I said quietly, "they say the hearing is the last to go."

So we took advantage of it. We talked to him out loud, sharing our hearts with him as we babbled on.

At first I told him how great it was to spend time with him at the Cape that summer and how much I had loved having him as a little brother. I reminded him of taking him on my dates and thanked him for giving me away at my wedding. I told him how much my kids loved him and how much they loved to hear Uncle Art tell our "poor stories" of growing up.

Eileen let him know she was there and how much she had loved growing up with him. She recalled her time with him that summer too and how she had especially loved chauffeuring him around the Cape in his convertible with the top down.

Linda expressed to him how much she loved his friendship and reminded him of how they had met at Pufferbellies and became instant friends. She let him know that he was the best "guy" friend she had ever had.

It seemed like we talked with him for hours as he lay with his eyes closed, quiet and calm in his bed. Each of us chimed in as the spirit hit us. We laughed, cried, and reminisced. Off and on, Art became restless and somewhat agitated. It almost seemed at one point he was anxious and wanted to get on with it. Whatever was going to happen, he was ready. Although he did not seem in pain, his breathing became more labored. I let him know we were there and whatever he decided was OK with us. I assured him that he had fought the good fight and that we were ready for whatever was to come. At one point, I told him that I had cashed his checks and that we would pay his bills. He was all set. I wanted him to know that we were there for him and could handle his affairs as needed. His breathing became intermittent, and each time he drew a big inhale, we all looked at each other as if to say, *Is this it?*

As it got harder for him to breathe, I continued to tell him that it was OK to go and that we were going to be OK—that we loved him and wished him well. It felt almost like we were helping him give birth, and maybe we were—birth to a new life.

"Quick, we need a Bible," said Eileen with a sense of desperation. Linda ran to the nurses' station and came back with a Bible, shutting the door to his room behind her.

"Look up the twenty-third Psalm. Let's read it together," I said as hot tears rolled down my cheeks.

Together we began:

The Lord is my Shepherd; I shall not want.

He maketh me to lie down in green pastures; he leadeth me beside the still waters.

He restoreth my soul; he leadeth me in the paths of righteousness for his name's sake.

Yea, though I walk through the valley of the shadow of death, I will fear no evil; for thou art with me; thy rod and thy staff comfort me.

Thou prepares a table before me in the presence of mine enemies.

Thou anoints my head with oil; my cup runneth over.

Surely goodness and mercy shall follow me all the days of my life; and I will dwell in the house of the Lord forever.

Linda put the Bible down on the bed. The three of us joined hands, and as we said the Lord's Prayer, Art took his last breath.

Out of nowhere, I felt a gentle breeze from the window blow the flowered curtains up in the air and whisk across the room and out the sliders, which were partially opened. I can remember crying out, "There's music, there's music! Do you hear the music?" It sounded like beautiful celestial chimes. I never knew if anyone else heard the music that night...but I know that I did.

CHAPTER TWENTY-ONE

It was after midnight when Eileen and I left the hospice and headed back to Art's apartment in Hyannis. Reality and the emotional toll were setting in. It was a very quiet ride. I could already feel Art's loss in the pit of my stomach. I looked over at Eileen, riding in the passenger seat where Art had sat only yesterday. I could hear her deep sighs and she had that faraway look of someone deep in her thoughts. I knew that we were both exhausted. When we arrived back at Art's apartment, Alice's kitchen light was on. She must have heard us unlock the outer door, because there she was, standing in her doorway in her nightgown, terry cloth robe, and slippers. She took one look at us, stepped outside, opened her arms, and gathered us into a group hug.

"It's over," I said, crying on her shoulder.

"I had a feeling that it might be," she said, offering me a box of tissues. "I waited up for you girls. Would you like to come in for a cup of tea?" she said, holding the door open.

"Thank you," I said. "But I think we will head up to bed; we're pretty drained from it all."

"You know," she continued, "Art always lit up when he knew you were coming for a visit, especially this summer. He loved you girls and your other sister so much. I really think he wanted you to be with him when he passed. And you were. Now, why don't you two get some sleep, and we'll talk tomorrow."

"Thanks Alice," we said almost in unison.

Eileen and I slowly made our way up the stairs and flopped down on the couches. I could feel the emptiness in the room without Art there. We had talked about it on the way home and knew we had to make one call that night. It was to Heather. Even though they had divorced earlier that year, she had been there for Art throughout his illness. She didn't seem surprised at the news, as we had kept her updated that night on Art's condition when we were at the hospice. She encouraged us to get some sleep and said she would touch base the next day and help us with anything we needed. We were grateful for her offer and promised to connect the next day.

"We have a lot to do tomorrow. Should we make more calls tonight or wait till morning?" I asked Eileen.

"You know, it's very late, almost 1:00 a.m., so why don't we try and get some sleep and take it all on in the morning," yawned Eileen.

"OK, but first I want to take a look at the sky before we go to bed. Let's go out on the balcony," I said.

As we glanced out over the trees at a clear, starlit night, there it was...just as I had hoped. One star, shining brighter than all the others.

"So long, Art…may God speed you on your way. You will always be in our hearts." This was all I could manage to get out.

"Love you, Art," whispered Eileen. Arm in arm, looking like Winnie the Pooh and Piglet, we made our way back inside and fell into our beds.

We both woke up early the next morning, and after a quick breakfast and cup of tea, we made a list of friends and family that we would have to call. Our sister Charlotte's husband, Bob, was on top of the list. We knew that he would want to contact Charlotte in Europe right away, as she was on a three-week trip and would want to fly home. We continued down the list of family to call. Each of us took a turn at telling the news of Art's passing. Then we called a few of Art's friends at the Cape and asked them to spread the word. As promised, Heather called us and said she would be happy to help us with the arrangements. We were so thankful for her help, as we knew she had lived on the Cape her whole life and would know who to call. Heather contacted the John-Lawrence Funeral Home in Marstons Mills. They got back to us right away and helped us begin the process of making arrangements for Art's funeral. Since we had little money to work with, they recommended we contact Mosswood Cemetery nearby in Cotuit. I called and reached a representative right away, and she informed me that if I could prove that Art had been a resident of the county for over two years, and if I could provide a signed residency verification, Art would qualify for a cemetery lot for a small fee.

I wrote a letter and Art's landlord, Alice, signed it, verifying that he had lived in Hyannis for over two years. In just a few hours, we were granted a cemetery lot at Mosswood for Art, and things moved quickly from there.

The phone never stopped ringing with calls from family and friends. Several of Art's friends dropped off food and flowers. Eileen and I proceeded to do what we did best: be there for Art. We wanted his funeral to be a tribute to him and his gracious battle.

We decided that memorial donations in Art's name could be made to Hospice House in Barnstable, or The Art Westfall Fund. We ordered a spray of Cape Cod flowers for his casket. We wanted something that was native to the area and looked just like the Cape...Art's Cape. We settled on bright blue bachelor buttons, hot pink beach roses, daisies, and lots of sea grass. The funeral director asked us to bring clothes for Art to be waked in. So once again, we had to pick out an outfit for Art. Eileen and I went through his closet and looked at different options: a black suit, a navy blazer, Hawaiian shirts, tuxedo shirts, and vests. None of these seemed to feel right. Then at the same time, we found it! We looked at each other and giggled like two little girls.

"Yes, this will be perfect!" I shouted.

"Let's do it!" exclaimed Eileen as we high-fived each other.

We chose a casual, long-sleeved striped dress shirt and a pair of really nice dress Bermuda shorts. That was Art's look. And, after all, no one would know, because we were going to have a closed casket. We decided to leave the collar open and add his gold chain necklace. Finally, we agreed on one more thing: we just had to do it. His best leather flip-flops. That was Art.

Next, we needed someone to officiate a service. Since Art

was not affiliated with a local church, we once again called upon the funeral director for suggestions. He directed us to the Cotuit Federated Church, which was right down the street from the cemetery. I called the minister, Rev. Elizabeth Endicott, and she agreed to do the service.

She asked to meet us so she would know something about Art. I invited her to come to Art's apartment. She came that evening, and to our surprise, she looked like she could be one of our sisters, with strawberry hair and freckles too. We instantly bonded as she gathered information about Art, which she would share in the service at his funeral.

The arrangements were made. The next day, the family arrived and convened at Art's place: our stepfather Gus, our children (Art's nieces and nephews), and our brothers-in-law. Art's apartment was soon full of people and quickly became a lot smaller. I knew that I wanted to write a eulogy for Art, so I gathered some paper and pens and sequestered myself in the walk-in attic, which was through a door right off his living room. I found it too distracting and noisy from all the people coming and going, so I grabbed a towel and headed to the beach. I wasn't there long when I saw Eileen coming down the path with a beach towel and pillow under her arm. She was crying her eyes out.

"What's up?" I asked, concerned.

"I can't be up there," she said. "Gus took a shower and now he's wearing Art's aftershave. I just can't stand it. That was Art's signature fragrance and he can't have it!"

"OK, OK," I said. "I get it. I'll tell him when I go back up to the house." Art had worn Old Spice aftershave lotion for years and we had always loved how manly he smelled. "Look, we're both overtired; let's just take a beach nap and I'll take care of it later," I said, trying to comfort her.

"Good idea. I brought my pillow," she managed to answer. And so we napped on the beach, wrapped in the comfort of the smell of the salt water in the air and the sound of the waves lapping in the background.

CHAPTER TWENTY-TWO

We only had one more day until the viewing and then the funeral. I still hadn't been able to bring myself to write Art's eulogy. I finally decided I'd try to take a walk on Art's beach just down the end of his street. So I gathered a sweatshirt, my sunglasses, a spiral binder, a few personal cards that Art had received, a couple of pens, and a bottle of water. I made my way down the familiar path to the beach. *This time I'm going to do it,* I told myself. It was early morning and the beachgoers had not yet arrived. I was grateful I had the beach all to myself. The sky was a brilliant blue with only a few wispy clouds. A gentle breeze guided me as I walked along the edge of the water. Of course, I couldn't resist picking up just a few more shells.

After walking quite a distance past the breakwater along Veterans Beach, without realizing it, I was almost to Kalmus Beach. I had walked further than I'd ever walked along this beach before. I turned around and made my way back. As I crossed the Hyannis

Yacht Club walkway, I noticed a beautiful grassy area up ahead on a hill above the Veterans Park Beach. I could see a flagpole with an American flag flapping in the breeze. So I decided to check it out. Much to my surprise, I found myself at the John F. Kennedy Memorial. With all the times I had walked on this beach, I had never stopped to see this beautiful spot. There was a simple memorial with a natural-cut stone wall boasting a large circular copper emblem with an engraved profile of President Kennedy. On the other side of the wall was a similar-sized copper emblem of the seal of the President of the United States. I gazed out over the rolling hill I had just climbed and could see a breathtaking view of Lewis Bay. I later learned that in his youth, President Kennedy often sailed in these waters when he visited the Kennedy Compound nearby in Hyannis Port. I noticed there were several granite benches nicely placed along the well-groomed paths throughout the small park. I suddenly felt calm and serene, and I knew that this was the place to write the eulogy. I chose a bench off to the side, sat down, and began…

> *Today we come together to share a "Celebration of Life."*
> *The life of our brother, Art Westfall.*
> *He was son to Ma and stepson to Gus.*
> *He was Uncle Art to Scott, Randy, Kent, Julie, Jamie, Jen, Matt, Jeff, Christy, Mike, and Louie.*
> *He was former husband to Heather and stepfather to Mike, Matt, and Tim.*
> *And a special friend to all of you.*

The words flowed, so I kept writing. I stayed there until I

finished and was satisfied with the eulogy. I knew I had done the best that I could for Art. I was so happy that I had brought a few of the many cards that Art received from his friends. This one gave me the support and courage to sum up what I was feeling:

> *Dear Art,*
> *How can we begin to put into words the feelings we hold deep in our hearts for you? You have shared your life with us. We will always remember you for your loving, giving heart and for the very, very special friend that you are to us. Please Artie, know how much we love you. May it help to comfort you and give you peace. Take our love and hold it in your heart, just as we will always feel and remember our love for you.*

Feeling thankful that I'd completed the eulogy, I made my way back down the grassy hill. Once again, I walked along the water's edge back to Art's apartment. I smiled to myself as our mother's old saying came to me. Today there truly was enough "blue in the sky to make a Dutchman's pants." Although we never understood that saying, I like to think that what she meant was: On a beautiful blue-sky day, all is right in the world.

CHAPTER
TWENTY-THREE

"It's time to go," I said.

Those of us who had gathered at Art's apartment made our way down the stairs and into our cars. We were on our way to Art's wake at the John-Lawrence Funeral Home in Marstons Mills. The rest of the family would meet us at the funeral home as soon as they arrived at the Cape. We wanted to be there early to see Art and to settle in. Eileen and I had requested a private, family-only viewing before the public viewing, as Art had lost so much weight and just didn't look like himself. When we actually got to see him, much to our surprise and delight, he looked great. Eileen and I looked at each other in disbelief. We hugged, and with a sigh of relief and happy tears we decided we wanted to share him with everyone. So we left the casket open. Our spray of Cape Cod wildflowers covered the lower half of the handsome, polished wooden casket. It was just as we had hoped—bright, colorful flowers and plenty of sea grass. Eileen and I looked at each other again with a mischievous twinkle in our eyes and a grin on our faces. No one knew our secret…Art was wearing his favorite striped shirt and Bermuda shorts.

We were anxious to see our sister Charlotte. Within an hour after she had received the call from her husband with the news of Art's passing, she had rearranged her travel plans and was on her way home from Rome and her European vacation. When Charlotte arrived, we had just enough time for a Westfall sisters hug before we formed a receiving line beside Art's casket for the viewing to begin. Friends from near and far streamed into the room, walking slowly past Art's casket. Several stopped, kneeled, and prayed. Most wiped tears as they introduced themselves to us and offered condolences to our family. Many had something special to say about Art, which touched our hearts and kept the tears flowing. One woman shared with me that Art had always been such a gentleman and that he had often taken time to walk her to her car in the darkened parking lot after a night of dancing at Pufferbellies. Another said she had always looked forward to seeing him at the club, especially recently when she knew that he had been diagnosed with pancreatic cancer and he was not always feeling well. As the line continued, it became evident that Art, just by being Art, had brought pure joy to so many. He had a way of making each and every one feel special.

Our kids, "the cousins," arrived. As they made their way through the line, they all looked freshly groomed and were dressed in their Sunday best. I hugged each of them and asked the same questions: "When did you get here? And where did you change?"

That became the family joke…they all had changed either in their trucks, in the back seat of their cars, or behind the dumpster! Art would have loved to hear those stories.

As the evening went on, I just couldn't keep the secret any longer. I had to tell someone, and I knew who it would be—my son Jeff. I knew that he would love it. So with a tilt of my head, I motioned him aside and whispered in his ear. "Guess what," I said. "Uncle Art is wearing his favorite Bermuda shorts and his best leather flip-flops." We had a great laugh together and for the rest of the night, whenever I caught Jeff's eye, he couldn't help but grin.

After the last guests left, we finished the evening with a family gathering at Art's apartment. We comforted each other as we laughed and cried, sharing our favorite stories of Art.

After much storytelling, we were all a little shocked when Charlotte announced she was going back to Europe the next day, right after the service. We understood when she told us why she had made that decision. She had met a very nice woman on the airplane on her way home from Italy. She shared with this stranger that she had left a vacation in Europe to go home for her brother's funeral. As they talked and cried together, her seatmate, and now new friend, convinced Charlotte to go back to Europe after the funeral and finish her trip. She said, "You have your whole life to grieve, and you may only have this one opportunity for a wonderful travel experience. Go back." And so she decided to fly back to Rome and finish her trip.

Before the evening ended, we asked "the boy cousins" (actually young men), Scott, Randy, Kent, Jeff, and Louie, to be pallbearers for Uncle Art. They were honored and thrilled to be chosen to do it. All we had left to do was prepare ourselves for our final goodbye.

The next day, on a crystal-clear, blue-sky day, we gathered at the funeral home to celebrate Art's life. The room had been rearranged from the previous night's viewing and was set up for the service. The casket and a small wooden lectern were at the front of the room with rows of folding chairs for the guests facing it. When all the guests were seated, the Rev. Elizabeth Endicott welcomed everyone. She offered a prayer and began her eulogy:

"I didn't personally know Art, but from what I've been told, it's an understatement to say he was well liked and well respected—and a wild and crazy guy. He was also a man who had an amazing ability to make and maintain friendships, something which was evident to me from the stories told about him and the pictures which were displayed here last night.

"Those of you who were here at the funeral home for visiting hours and who have been in his apartment know of those pictures, and also of the mementos he kept around him. All of them captured a special event in his life and reminded him of people he enjoyed. One picture showed his nieces and nephews huddled around him, all of them with huge grins on their faces and each wearing one of his coveted baseball caps—the same caps which hung from the rafters in his apartment, each representing another special event in his life: a trip, a game, a favorite brew. On the shelves of his china closet are other trinkets, treasures, and glasses from various establishments he frequented, all reminders, like those pictures, of him or his favorite people in a time

or place he didn't want to forget.

"Art was good at creating memories—parties with surprise guests or antics, visits with laid-back conversations or exciting adventures, jokes told at his expense, or stories shared and embellished into legends. I'm sure you all have your favorites and I hope you'll recall them later after the service. I understand many of them are best told by someone other than the minister...

"Although there are certainly many entertaining memories of him, perhaps some of the most valuable are how he dealt with his cancer and his impending death. From what I've gathered, he accepted them both, but he didn't let either defeat him. Through it all, he maintained as normal a lifestyle as possible—working and playing, sharing and caring as he always did, even right up to the end. Although the cancer changed his physique, it could not change his spirit.

"In such a time as this, when we're here to celebrate the life of a great guy, we also can't help but ask the 'Why?' questions. Why did one so young and so vibrant have to die so soon? Why him? Why that way? I can't answer those questions, because we'll never know the reasons for certain, but I can ask you to listen to these words from the Gospel of John, chapter eleven, verses twenty-one through twenty-seven, for the hope they give us: 'Martha said to Jesus, "Lord, if you had been here, my brother would not have died. But even now I know that God will give you whatever you ask of him." Jesus said to her, "Your brother will rise again." Martha said to him, "I know that he will rise in the resurrection on the last day." Jesus said to her, "I am the resurrection and the life. Those who believe, even though they die, will live, and everyone who lives and believes in me will never die. Do you believe* *this?" She said to him, "Yes Lord, I believe that you are the Messiah, the Son of God, the one coming in the world."'*

"And that is a terrific lesson for all. No matter what struggles we face in life, no matter what faith we have or don't have, we all will do well to face them as Art did: with courage and acceptance and determination, taking them in stride and willing to go on, making the best of the situation, whatever it may be. His was a wonderful attitude to have, and in tribute to him, we all can benefit by adopting it, no matter how well we knew him.

"Art's sisters, Charlotte, Marylin, and Eileen, have prepared a special tribute to their brother, which I invite them now to share with you."

The three of us made our way to the front of the room and stood by Art's casket. I had convinced my sisters to stand there with me for support as I read the eulogy that I had written just the day before on a hilltop overlooking the beach at Lewis Bay. With a lump in my throat, I began:

"Today we come together to share a 'Celebration of Life.' The life of our brother, Art Westfall.

"First, as Art's family, we would like to thank you for coming today to celebrate Art. We want to thank you not only for your loving support for Art, but your support for us over the past few months. We've gotten to know many of you and now you are not only Art's friends, but you are our friends. You will always be in our hearts.

"We also want to thank Rev. Elizabeth Endicott for her kind

and inspiring words."

I paused, took a deep breath, and read the eulogy.

"He was son to Ma and stepson to Gus. He was Uncle Art to Scott, Randy, Kent, Julie, Jamie, Jen, Matt, Jeff, Christy, Mike, and Louie. He was former husband to Heather and stepfather to Mike, Matt, and Tim. And a special friend to all of you.

"Artie, or 'Ottie' as so many of you with a Massachusetts accent knew him, was the youngest of the four of us and the apple of our mother's eye. As youngsters, we grew up on the Milford, Connecticut, shoreline. The four of us were inseparable and watched out for each other all the time. We spent a lot of time playing at the beach. Art spent a good part of his childhood underwater, so it doesn't surprise us that he ended up at Cape Cod, surrounded by water.

"Art was a good athlete. He played many sports, including being a standout pitcher in Little League baseball, and then went on to letter in three sports in high school: football, baseball, and basketball. In his senior year, he was awarded the coveted William Savitt award. This was an honor voted on by his teammates. It was given for Outstanding Sportsmanship and Personality. I am sure that this does not surprise any of you.

"Art loved to laugh, had a great sense of humor, and could tell a funny story better than anyone I know. After high school, Art learned the finance business and was in the 'shirt and tie world' for several years, until one winter after he was recently divorced. He went to Mount Snow, Vermont, to ski with friends. He ended up staying there to work and play (probably mostly play). There he learned to be a bartender and never went back to the corporate world again. To

borrow a phrase from Frank Sinatra, 'Art did life his way.'

"*At the end of ski season that year, Art came to work (and play) at the Cape and has made this his home ever since. Those who knew him well bet 'Party Artie' wouldn't make it till Labor Day in this vacation atmosphere. But he did and has been here for fifteen years.*

"*Art loved his cocktails, loved people, and loved to party. I'm sure some of you could tell us a few Artie stories. I think I even heard that he invented the Sandal Shot. Art's work in the food and beverage industry soon became his way of life. He loved what he did, and he did it well. His work and play were one and the same until about one month ago.*

"*Art never had children of his own, but he loved sharing Heather's boys, Mike, Matt, and Tim. He treated them like they were his own. Through them, he had a chance to be a kid again—bodysurfing, fishing, and watching them play sports. Heather and Art have remained good friends, and she and the boys helped care for him till the end.*

"*What I wanted most was to share with you today what we learned from Art about courage, love, and friendship. As most of you know, Art was diagnosed with pancreatic cancer a little over a year ago. He underwent a major exploratory operation to no avail. Then radiation and chemotherapy, which was no easy task. He faced his illness with courage, taking one step at a time.*

"*At this point, we began to see something magical happen: Art came home more often, rekindling friendships with family and friends. Everyone began to surround him with their love and support. His lifelong friends from Milford threw parties and intimate dinners in his honor. A group of special friends here at the Cape organized a benefit fundraiser to help him in his battle for life. We sisters came to the Cape more frequently and the four of us became closer than ever again. All our children, 'the cousins,' came from near and far to share their love for Uncle Art. Heather and her boys came back into Art's life. His landlords, Alice and Bob, looked out for him.*

"And all his local friends and work associates did everything they could to support him. He even had his own very special guardian angel. We all wanted to be there for him.

"I once got an opportunity to thank Art's oncologist—or 'poisonologist,' as Art affectionately called him—for everything he'd done for Art. He answered that through Art's courage, Art had given him much more than he had done for Art.

"It seemed to me that Art's only wishes were simple: that he be able to work as long as possible, be able to stay in his apartment with a water view which he loved so much, and, mostly, that he not be a burden to anyone. I believe that he accomplished those goals, and through everyone's love and support, Art outlived all the expectations for someone with pancreatic cancer.

"I truly believe that it was his attitude and the love that surrounded him that gave us this extra time with him. Even till the very end, we got more from him than we could have ever possibly given to him."

When I finished reading my eulogy, the three of us together, the Westfall sisters, with tears rolling down our cheeks, read the Irish Blessing:

May the road rise to meet you.
May the wind be always at your back.
May the sunshine warm up your face.
May the rain fall soft upon your fields.
And until we meet again, may God hold you in the palm
   of His hand.

This concluded the service, and we made our way back to our seats.

The family remained seated as friends and guests said their goodbyes to Art and made their way out.

To my surprise and delight, a couple of people stopped to say something to me.

The first was Dr. Brown, Art's oncologist. As he walked past me, he stopped to give an affectionate squeeze to my shoulder. He offered his condolences and gave me a wink. It meant so much to know that he thought so much of Art, that he took time from his busy practice to come to the service. I'm not sure many doctors do that.

And then I saw the woman with our mother's beautiful crystal-blue eyes. She was the nurse's aide from the hospice. I couldn't believe she had come to the service. She reached over, gave me a hug, and whispered in my ear, "I am so glad that you stayed to be with your brother that night. Thank you for letting me be a part of something so beautiful." With a lump in my throat, I could only say, "Thank you."

When it was the family's turn to say our goodbyes and take

Art to his final resting place, a special thought came to me. I whispered in Eileen's ear and when she nodded in agreement, I asked the funeral director to remove the gold necklace that Art was wearing. I knew just who we would give it to—Linda, the special friend who had been his guardian angel during his illness and who had been there with us the night he passed.

CHAPTER
TWENTY-FOUR

Our family was the last to say our goodbyes to Art and then we left the funeral home to form a procession to Mosswood Cemetery in Cotuit. Before we got into our cars, we all said a tearful goodbye to Charlotte as she headed off to the airport to fly back to Rome, where she would join her group and continue her travels in Europe. I know this was not an easy decision for her, and difficult timing, but it was the right one for sure.

I was sitting in my car, prepared to join the procession, when a woman who was leaving the service stopped by my car, and through the open window, handed me a piece of paper. Holding back her tears she said, "Here, I wrote this for Art, and I want you to have it." I thanked her and because we were waiting in line, I had a chance to read it:

Art Westfall
Your journey has been long and now the end.
Your life has been fun and rich with love.
Your friends have been many and warm and kind.
Enriched by the example you've left behind.
Go with joy to a better place and a new beginning.
Go in peace and know that you've made a difference along
*   the way.*
Go in comfort, for all you've been remains to stay!
Joann Wright

Just when I thought I did not have another tear left in me, down the cheeks they came again. I had no idea how long the ride would take from Marstons Mills to the cemetery in Cotuit, so I went on automatic pilot and followed the cars ahead of me. We took a right out of the funeral home onto Route 28, then a quick left onto Putnam Avenue. It was only about one and a half miles. In what seemed like just a blink of an eye, we were entering through the ornate iron gates into Mosswood Cemetery. I was struck by the peaceful setting of sweeping green hills and ornamental trees. I noticed that there were no upright monuments or headstones. Having no landscape distractions made it feel all the more serene. When we got out of our cars at what would be Art's resting place, I heard the chirping of birds and the tinkling of wind chimes hung in the trees. There it was...beautiful celestial music again. I felt at ease and knew that this was the place for Art.

After a short graveside service lead by Rev. Endicott, I read a poem that I had read only a little more than a year before at our mother's graveside, where I had stood holding Art's hand just a month before he was diagnosed:

> *Do not stand at my grave and weep.*
> *I am not there. I do not sleep.*
> *I am a thousand winds that blow.*
> *I am the diamond glints on snow.*
> *I am the sunlight on ripened grain.*
> *I am the gentle autumn rain.*
> *When you awaken in the morning's hush,*
> *I am the swift uplifting rush of quiet birds in circling flight.*
> *I am the soft star that shines at night.*
> *Do not stand at my grave and cry.*
> *I am not there. I did not die.*
> *—Anonymous*

It was over. It wasn't a Viking funeral with a lighted funeral pyre set out to sea, as Art had requested with that familiar twinkle in his eye, but we had done our best.

Now, time to move on to what Art would have liked best, a gathering of his friends and family. It was time for Artie's Party. We were graciously invited for a repass reception at the home of Art's good friend, Debbie Morgan, who lived nearby in Marstons Mills. She not only offered to host the gathering at her home but she took charge of the planning. I was amazed to see the spread of food and drink—cheese and fruit platters, shrimp cocktail, scallops wrapped in bacon, salads, baked beans, coleslaw, and an abundance of desserts, all donated by Sophie's, Good Fellows, The Black Cat, Kerrigan's, and Mildred's, to name a few, and I am sure there were others. Plus there also was a big pot of Spanky's famous clam chowder. I guess I should not have been so surprised that many of the local restaurants, bars, and beverage companies were only too happy to donate the refreshments. That's what people in the hospitality industry do: they take care of each other.

We, Art's family, did not stay too long. We had a bite to eat, thanked the hostess, and left the partying to Art's friends. Before we left the reception, we had one more thing to do: we wanted to give Art's youngest stepson, Tim, who was now a teenager of sixteen, Art's gold pinky ring, which Art had worn for years. It was a simple, soft gold, well-worn signet ring with Art's initials barely visible. I am not sure if Art had promised the ring to Tim, but we knew he would have wanted him to have it. Eileen and I found Tim among the crowd of people. We called him aside and gave him the ring. Tim shyly accepted the gift and thanked us.

On our way out of the party, Debbie Morgan caught up with us and told us she had something for the Westfall sisters. The Art Westfall Foundation committee had decided they were going to pay for an extra month's rent on Art's apartment so the sisters could have some time to enjoy the Cape. She said they knew that we had spent months caring for Art and they had decided Art would love this for us. We were shocked, delighted, and overwhelmed to say the least. We thanked her, promised to keep in touch, and once again said our goodbyes.

It was time for all of us, Art's family, to go our separate ways. Time to go home, but knowing that we would be back. For me, in my heart, I knew that the Cape, with its beaches, bars, restaurants, and vacation lifestyle, would always belong to Art. And it still does.

When a few of us went back to Art's apartment to pack our things, I noticed more cards, which Alice, the landlord, had left on the table. And sure enough, there was one that brought the tears flowing again. It came from the staff of the Radiation Therapy Center where Art had undergone chemo and radiation treatments, and read:

> *We all loved Arthur here—he was a gentle man who not only fought his disease with quiet courage, but also sought to ease the fears of fellow patients he encountered.*
> *We share your sorrow and loss.*
> *The Staff at Radiation Therapy*

And another from one of his dear friends who included this special reading:

A Comrade Rides Ahead
Time brings not death, it brings but changes;
I know he rides, but rides afar,
Today some other planet ranges
And camps tonight upon a star
Where his other comrades are.
Whatever vales we yet may wander
What sorrow come, what tempest blow,
We have a friend, a friend out yonder,
To greet us when we have to go—
Out yonder someone that we know.
To all eternity he binds us;
He links the planet and the star;
He rides ahead, the trail he finds us
And where he is and where we are
Will never seem again so far.
By: Douglas Malloch

Physically, mentally, and emotionally depleted, Eileen and I decided that we would read more of the cards when we came back to the Cape in the next couple of weeks.

For now, it was time to be on our way home. Home to the lives we had left behind.

CHAPTER TWENTY-FIVE

Two weeks after Art's funeral, we were trying to get back into our own lives, but Eileen and I decided that it was time to go back to the Cape and clean out Art's apartment. We agreed to meet there on Friday afternoon and spend the weekend. Since Charlotte was still on her European vacation, we felt that she would just have to trust our judgment as to what to do with Art's belongings. Although the two of us drove from different parts of Connecticut, we planned to arrive at just about the same time. We had agreed to meet in the driveway and go into Art's apartment together. It had only been a couple weeks since we had seen each other, but when we got out of our cars, we hugged like it had been years. We had always been close, but now we shared a bond like no other. We had been there, together, to help Art die.

I said, "Ready?"

She said, "As ready as I will ever be."

We made our way up the stairs to Art's apartment. Opening the door brought back a rush of memories of all the times we had spent there with Art, both the fun times before he was sick and the times that we were there helping him as he courageously battled pancreatic cancer. Although everything was just as we had left it, the apartment felt empty. Something was missing, and that something was Art. We both immediately crossed the room and headed for the balcony, which was our favorite part of his apartment. I remembered the many times I would escape out there so Art would not see me crying, and I also remembered the many times when Eileen would call me for support as she was crying on the balcony when she was caring for Art. As I opened the slider to step out, a wonderful sea breeze rushed in, carrying the smell of the salt water in the air. I felt like I was home again...a different home, but nonetheless a feeling of home. I leaned on the railing and stared out at the great view of the bay.

I said, "You know, this is not going to be easy."

She replied, "I know, but I'm glad that we're doing it together."

"Me too," I answered.

We eventually made our way back inside to have a look around. The old orange-and-gold crocheted throw was still draped over Art's leather recliner, right where he had left it. When we opened all the shades and windows to let the sunlight in, I noticed that the baskets of Cape Cod wildflowers from Art's funeral were still sitting on the coffee table, now faded, wilted, and totally dried out. I remembered how beautiful they had been when we'd left them there, not realizing we wouldn't be back to enjoy them for a couple of weeks. So that's where we began. We gathered the wilted flowers and began our first bag of trash, but of course saved the baskets, because that's what the Westfall sisters do. As I continued to look around, I remembered we had left some unopened cards on the kitchen table. Alice had also left some more recent mail, including a few cards addressed to the Westfall sisters in care of Art's address. So we sat and opened them. The first was a sympathy card that read:

"Those we hold most dear never truly leave us…they live on in the kindnesses they showed, the comfort they shared, and the love they brought into our lives."

On the left side of the card, there was a lovely handwritten note that read:

You all did a great job at the funeral sharing your memories with us. We all have our own special thoughts of Artie. He was loved by many. We will always remember him. I have enjoyed getting to know all of you a little too.
My thoughts and prayers are with you,
Jane Valine

After reading a few more cards, I realized how much receiving a personal note and/or a sympathy card means to those close to the person who has passed. I vowed going forward to make sure that I chose cards with a heartfelt message and to always write a personal note. After reading the rest of the cards and sharing a box of tissues, we knew we had to move on.

"OK," I said. "Let's do the easy things first."

Eileen agreed and she said, "Let's do the things we weren't attached to."

So the refrigerator was first. Out went the mustard, ketchup, some grape jelly, a block of cheese, and a couple of bottles of beer. Then we moved on to the food in the cabinets, only saving the nonperishable items to donate to a food pantry. Things became a little bit more real as we moved on to clean the bathroom. When I opened the door, the sweet smell hit me, the manly fragrance of Irish Spring soap. "Oh my God, it smells like Art in here," I said. Eileen did her best to hold it together until we got to the medicine cabinet. In it was Art's special Old Spice aftershave.

"How are we going to do this?" Eileen said as she burst into tears.

It was then that we reconfirmed that it wasn't going to be easy to clean out Art's stuff. We also knew that we had to do it. We forged on ahead. Next came the wall decor. Art's collection of baseball caps hanging on pegs and hooks were all around the room. The caps helped boost our spirits as we decided to each choose our favorite one to keep. Mine was a light blue denim with an orange-and-yellow embroidered Kahlua logo. This was one of his favorites and is now one of mine. Eileen chose one that she loved, a khaki cap with a lime-green iguana embroidered on the front. We tried them on, smiled at each other, and knew that we had found strength to continue. It seemed like we took hours choosing the perfect hat for each niece, nephew, and brother-in-law. This was a labor of love and I felt Art was right there with us, enjoying choosing the perfect cap for each person. Next we decided to empty his glass-enclosed bookcase. We found an empty shoebox to store the tchotchkes that he had picked up along the shore as he walked the nearby beaches. Among his beach finds were matchbox cars, a rubber crab, and a troll with bright orange hair, wearing a bandanna and a cowboy hat.

As we continued to empty the shelves, we dusted and boxed his sports awards and trophies. And then we found a real treasure: a five-page list of ingredients for popular cocktail drinks and specialty coffees. Not only was it handwritten, but it was also in alphabetical order. Well, at least we thought it was a treasure. We decided we would have to think about who would enjoy this find.

We knew we still had another day to do more sorting and packing, so we decided to take a break and walk down to Hyannis Harbor for dinner. We didn't realize what a walk down memory lane it would be until we got near the docks. We realized it when we saw some of Art's favorite restaurants: The Black Cat, Harborview, Spanky's, and The Mooring. These were the places he frequented and sat at the bar for dinner most nights. We looked at each other and agreed that we just couldn't go into one of these restaurants—not that night, anyway. We got two hot dogs from a vendor on the dock and sat on a nearby bench, where we watched a beautiful sunset and the ferries as they came and went out of the harbor to the nearby islands.

The next morning, we started early. By now we had a pile of remembrances for each of the immediate family members and we were ready to take on Art's closet of clothes to share those too. As I have mentioned before, Art was a great dresser. We sisters loved borrowing his cool clothes, so we knew this would be fun. We divided up the Hawaiian shirts, Oxford button-down shirts with "Pufferbellies" tastefully embroidered over the pockets, windbreakers, and lots of T-shirts. We made sure that everyone received something special.

Eileen and I spent most of the day sorting and packing. We stopped to reminisce about his high school days and remembered what a great athlete he had been. Just when we thought we were about done, we found his high school letter sweaters from the sixties, like the ones Richie wore on the popular TV show *Happy Days*. There was a maroon-and-white one from Milford High School, boasting an emblem for varsity baseball, which he earned in his sophomore year. There was also a white letter sweater trimmed in black and gold from the new Jonathan Law High School, which had opened across town during Art's junior year. He excelled in sports, both at Milford High School and then Jonathan Law. He earned varsity letters for football, basketball, and baseball. We treasure those sweaters, and they are still stored by our nephew, Randy, who is keeper of our family photos and memorabilia.

Each time we took a break, we headed out to our usual spot on the balcony. I looked out over the familiar view of the harbor and I saw it: the Cat Boat in full sail! I nudged Eileen and pointed to it. We looked at each other and without saying a word, we both knew exactly what we were going to do.

"Let's go," I said.

We ran down the stairs, jumped in my car, and headed for the harbor. The next available time was for a sunset cruise that night. We booked the last two seats on the Cat Boat and headed back to Art's place to get ready. As we came around the garage, I saw Alice and Bob, Art's landlords, relaxing in their yard, enjoying the beautiful Cape Cod day. We had been wanting to talk with them, but subconsciously, we were dreading and avoiding a final conversation. We knew eventually we would have to say goodbye.

"Hey, girls. Come join us for some lemonade," shouted Alice.

"Thanks, we'd love to," I said.

Alice quickly disappeared inside, returning with four frosted mugs of lemonade and a plate of her famous chocolate chip cookies. As we sat at their umbrella table by the creek, I couldn't help but feel the unspoken loss in the air. Alice finally addressed the elephant in the room by remarking, "You know, we miss him too. We liked Art a lot and loved getting to know all about him in your eulogy at the funeral."

"He liked you too and loved living here," I said.

Bob, who had always been so quiet, added, "Yeah, a real nice fellow. Never gave us any trouble and always paid his rent on time...and in cash too."

With a lump in my throat, I finally got the courage to say, "We're cleaning out the apartment, but we don't know what to do with the furniture. Do you have any interest?"

They looked at each other and thankfully agreed that they would keep the furniture and rent the space as a furnished apartment to the next tenant.

Now that we had gotten that out of the way, Eileen spoke up and said, "If it's OK with you, we'll be back next weekend with our sister Charlotte to finish cleaning the apartment, and we'll give you the keys when we leave."

"Of course, that will be fine," said Alice. "We'll look forward to seeing you girls again next weekend, and don't hesitate to ask if there's anything else we can do."

"Thanks," I said. "Now we have to go get ready for our sail tonight. We're going on the Cat Boat!"

"Oh, that sounds like so much fun," Alice replied. "Enjoy."

Eileen and I ran up the stairs, happy to change the subject and get ready for the evening. We each put on our newly chosen baseball caps from Art's collection, took a couple of his windbreakers, and walked back to the harbor for our evening sail.

I reminded Eileen that this was the cruise that I had always wanted to go on with Art. But sadly, he became too weak to do it.

Since it was August 24, Eileen's birthday, and mine had been just the day before on August 23, we agreed this sunset cruise was a gift from Art. As we sailed out of Hyannis Harbor on a perfect summer evening, we both knew this was a gift we would never forget.

CHAPTER TWENTY-SIX

I t was now the last weekend of August, and Art's apartment rental was about to run out. The Westfall sisters had been so grateful to The Art Westfall Foundation, who had generously rented the apartment for an extra month just for us. It gave us time to not only visit the Cape, but to clean out Art's apartment and finish any of Art's unfinished affairs, of which there were very little.

Charlotte was now back from her European vacation and so once again, "the girls," as Art liked to call us, converged on Cape Cod. Since the three of us had stayed with Art several times, we took over his apartment and easily settled in. We each had our favorite place to sleep—two in the single beds tucked in the corners on either side of the sliders to his balcony and one on the couch. Charlotte was very surprised at all the work that Eileen and I had already done in thoughtfully dividing up Art's stuff. We were mainly there to spend time with each other and to say goodbye to the Cape—at least, the Cape as we had known it that year...Art's Cape.

We enjoyed Friday evening together with Charlotte, sharing

stories of her vacation and all the countries she had visited, and Eileen and I sharing our stories of caring for Art. We continued to reminisce about our time at the Cape and relived Art's last night at the hospice. We told Charlotte about the burial service and how special the cemetery was, and we filled her in on the afterparty at the Morgans'. We took turns passing the tissue box around and managed to get through the evening together laughing and crying. There was no question; we were all missing Art.

Charlotte finally asked, "So what else do we have to do for Art this weekend?" Since Charlotte had left the Cape right after the funeral and had not gone to the cemetery, I said, "How about we make a visit to Art's grave first? We really want you to see the cemetery. I also made an appointment with a monument company for us to choose a headstone while we are all here together."

Eileen added, "And we want to show you the hospice house in Barnstable."

"OK," she said. "We have a plan for tomorrow. Let's say goodnight to the stars and get some rest."

After breakfast on Saturday morning, we took a walk on the nearby beach. Art's beach. It was the last weekend of summer, just before Labor Day, and the vacation crowds had not yet arrived that morning. We really had the beach almost all to ourselves. So the Westfall sisters took off our shoes and walked along the water's edge, reminiscent of the many times we had done this in our childhood growing up on the Connecticut shore. We knew that we were going to the cemetery that morning, so without even consulting each other, we each picked up a handful of shells and pretty rocks. When we returned to the apartment after our walk, we decided it was time to begin the rest of our day.

"Let's get started. I'll drive," I said.

First, we were off to Mosswood Cemetery in Cotuit to find Art's grave. On our way, we stopped at a garden center and picked up a small flowering potted plant. It wasn't long before we entered the familiar iron gates and drove slowly through the winding roads, trying to remember where Art's gravesite was. Eileen said, "All I remember is that it was on the left near a tree-lined area." I drove slowly as we continued to look, and suddenly, as if we had been guided, we came right to it. There it was, covered with fresh dirt. The beautiful Cape Cod wildflower spray that had graced his casket was now dried up and placed to one side. What made it real was a small brass post marker sticking in the ground with his name on it: Arthur Westfall. As I looked around, I still marveled at the beauty of this place. The quiet wooded border and the well-cared-for grounds added to the serenity. I found myself again drawn to the tinkling, melodious sounds of wind chimes and to the brightly colored painted birdhouses hanging in the trees. I cleaned off the top of the grave with my hand, smoothing out the dirt. Charlotte placed our small plant in the middle and we each carefully placed our pocket of shells and stones artfully around the plant. No words were needed. We stood there for a couple minutes in silence.

The three of us spontaneously held hands and encircled his grave. I uttered, "We miss you, Art. We'll be back."

We stayed for a little longer, not wanting to leave Art, until

Charlotte, who doesn't like to show her emotions, finally said, "Let's go. We have more work to do."

Our next stop was at Maki Monument in West Barnstable. We had an appointment to order a headstone for Art's grave. At this point, I think we were already numb and just going through the motions.

Mr. Maki, the kind owner, helped us choose a barre gray stone marker. Then he asked the hard question, "What do you want to say on it?"

We looked at each other like deer in headlights and fortunately, Charlotte spoke up. "How about 'Beloved Son, Brother, Uncle, Friend'?"

I said, "Sounds good to me," as I didn't have a better idea.

Eileen, holding back tears, silently nodded her head in agreement. Then Mr. Maki printed it out for our approval.

Arthur Dean Westfall
1947–1996
Beloved Son, Brother, Uncle, Friend

I wrote a check for the deposit, and we were done.

Mr. Maki thanked us and said, "I'll take good care of you girls, and we'll let you know when it's installed."

We thanked him and headed to my car. When all the car doors were shut, we breathed a collective sigh of relief.

Keeping us on task, as she does, Charlotte said, "Check… Where to next?"

"Well," I offered. "Might as well go to the hospice house; it's not far from here."

This was the one place that I was dreading, as it had only been a few short weeks since Eileen and I had driven Art there, not knowing that it would be his last day. I hardly remembered what the place looked like, as we had brought him there on a rainy afternoon and he'd died there the next night. We had a couple of missions here: first was to find the brick inscribed with Art's name on it in the hospice memorial garden walk. When we arrived at the hospice house, I parked my car, and we followed the brick walk around the side of the building that led through beautiful perennial gardens lined with hydrangeas still in bloom. We checked the names on the bricks as we went along, reading many of them out loud.

"Oh no," I said. "We have to stop doing this. Only old people read out loud."

We all burst out laughing as the Westfall sisters often do.

And then...there it was. A freshly installed brick with new soil packed around it:

Art Westfall from the Country Crowd at Pufferbellies

I bent down, gently touched the brick, and said, "They really loved him. He had so many friends."

After spending a few minutes in the garden, Eileen linked her arm with mine, looked at me with a caring glance, and whispered, "Are you going to be OK?"

We had spent Art's last night together here in this hospice helping him die. I felt those memories come flooding back.

"Are you sure you want to go inside? We don't have to," she said.

"I think so," I replied. "I'm as ready as I'll ever be."

To our surprise and delight, Nancy, one of Art's nurses who he affectionally called "babe," saw us come in and came to greet us. "So good to see you," she said, and gave each of us a hug.

I introduced Charlotte and said, "We're here to show our sister the memory books. OK if we do that?"

"Of course. Help yourselves and stay as long as you'd like."

We made our way into the cozy living room and there they were—a stack of scrapbooks sitting on the coffee table. We each picked one and began thumbing through it. While I didn't know if it would be too soon to expect it, there it was: Art's page. The page had his obituary from the newspaper and a spray of dried flowers under a clear plastic page cover. Even though we came looking for it, it was still hard to see.

Charlotte said, "Good thing we came prepared."

"I know," I replied, and began to rummage through my pocketbook.

I had brought a small plastic sandwich bag filled with mementos, just in case there was a page there for Art. There was our favorite photo of the four of us in Art's convertible, taken only last summer, a bookmark printed with the Irish Blessing, a few small shells from Art's beach, and of course, a dried bachelor button flower from his funeral spray of Cape Cod wildflowers. Charlotte did the arranging and made the page look beautiful. When we were satisfied, Eileen remarked, "Looks great, mission accomplished."

We high-fived each other and shared a mischievous Westfall grin, happy with our creative achievement. Art now had his own special page.

"Before we go," I said, "I want to take a walk around back and see the patio outside Art's room."

Something was calling me there, and when we came around the corner, I knew what it was. "The celestial music! I hear it! I hear it!" I squealed like a little girl hearing Santa's bells for the first time. It was then that I noticed the wind chimes hanging from a branch over the patio right outside the sliders to what had been Art's room. The chimes had beautiful long silver tubes held from a polished wooden heart with a colorful metal hummingbird hanging at the bottom. I remembered that the night Art passed, a gentle breeze had blown across his room, and I had heard music. I later thought that maybe I was making it up and only believed I had heard music. I now knew what it was. I think my heart will be forever touched when I hear wind chimes. I like to think it's an angel getting its wings.

"Time for a beach nap," Charlotte stoically announced. She was done with all this difficult emotional stuff. Eileen and I agreed. We drove back to Art's apartment, where we grabbed beach towels and pillows and headed to the beach. Later that night, as we were enjoying our last sunset from Art's balcony, I noticed three large birds floating in the creek right below us. At first I thought they were seagulls, but then I realized what they were. "Look, there they are! That's what we saw on the TV tonight," I shouted with joy. The three large birds were part of a flock of white pelicans that were just spotted at the Cape. We learned from the local news that white pelicans spend their summers in the north, but return each year to spend the fall, winter, and spring on the Gulf Coast. We stood there and observed them swimming around as the sun went down and the moon and stars came out. Eventually the three pelicans headed toward the open waters of Lewis Bay and took flight on their way home.

In that moment, the three of us knew that it was time for the Westfall sisters to go home too.

HEALING

The light in his eyes will no longer shine
and his voice is forever still,
But his love will always live in your heart
and your memories relived at will.
When someone you love dies and leaves you behind
the pain seems to never end,
But the darkness will lift to let sunshine return
and your heart will begin to mend.
Then you'll look at the past with a smile on your lips
and remember the days gone by,
When you made all those memories to hold in your heart
and your tears will begin to dry.
But for now, my dear friend, if you just need to talk
or share a bad day or two,
Please know that I'm here and I care very much
and I'll always be here for you.
You can speak of him then, say his name out loud
and I won't try to look away.

It's OK to remember the ones that we love
and to do it in our own way.
So shed all your tears and sigh all your sighs
and let all your feelings flow free,
And when you are ready to share all these things
you know you can share them with me.

Sue MacDonald
1996

A few weeks after Art's passing, I received this poem from a dear friend and sister-in-law who herself was in the last stages of breast cancer and passed shortly thereafter.

24 YEARS LATER...

I t was early summer 2020, the year of the beginning of the COVID-19 pandemic and before vaccines were available, that I decided to take a trip back to Cape Cod to do some research for this book. I had been thinking about doing this trip for several months. Finally, I decided I would do it with caution, no matter what the virus situation was.

I waited until late September to schedule my trip, as I knew the Cape would be less crowded, and I was hopeful it would still be warm enough that I could eat my meals outside. Remember, during the beginning of the pandemic, most people were not eating in restaurants—at least, I was not. I waited for a good weather forecast for the upcoming week. I searched the internet, and to my delight I found a little B&B inn, the Cape Cod Ocean Manor Inn, right on Ocean Street in Hyannis. Luck was with me, as they had a room available, so I knew this trip was meant to be. I was excited for this solo adventure.

The route was not quite as familiar, as I then resided in Middletown, a different area of Connecticut from when I had commuted to the Cape to spend time with Art so many years before. But I now had a cell phone with a Google Maps GPS program so that I didn't have to travel with written directions clutched in my hand. It was a beautiful autumn day for traveling, and before I knew it, I was once again crossing the Sagamore Bridge and on my way to the Hyannis Harbor area. I easily found the sweet little B&B. The location could not have been more perfect. It was just across the street from Veterans Memorial Park and Beach, a ten-minute walk to Hyannis Harbor, fifteen minutes from downtown Hyannis, and best of all…a short-distance walk to the street where Art had lived. I was welcomed by the owner, who assured me that the inn was following CDC protocols for cleaning, which put my mind at ease. I could feel myself begin to relax a little when he showed me my first-floor room with a slider to a beautiful deck overlooking a salt marsh, with a distant view of Nantucket Sound. It didn't take long for me to settle into my room. I grabbed my windbreaker and headed out for a walk to the harbor. I crossed a small bridge with a narrow creek running under it. I looked to where the water was going and recognized it was the creek that ran right past Art's backyard. I could actually see the house with the flagpole in the backyard and Art's small balcony over the garage. I thought about it, but I was not yet ready to walk down his street. I continued my walk to the harbor.

I found myself at home at Hyannis Harbor with the familiar restaurants: Spanky's, The Harborview, The Black Cat, and one of Art's favorites, The Mooring, which was now called The Landing. I went immediately to Spanky's for some clam chowder. The wind off the water had really picked up, but I was determined to eat outside. I had promised myself that I would only eat outdoors on this trip. I pulled the hood of my jacket up and hunkered down at a table as close to the building as I could. I laughed as I almost had to tie myself to my chair on the deck to keep from blowing away. I was the only one eating outside, but I made it happen.

It continued to be very windy along the harbor, but after my lunch, I took time to enjoy a stroll through Bismore Park to check out the colorful HyArts Artist Shanties. I had always loved meeting the local artists showcasing their wares of original handcrafted items, including unique jewelry and paintings. And of course, I bought yet another pair of sea glass earrings.

As the afternoon went on, the temperature dropped, and it was becoming chilly. I knew that the sun would be setting soon, so I began my walk back toward my B&B. This time, when I got to Harbor Bluff, Art's street, I took a quick walk past his apartment. I knew that Alice and Bob, his landlords, had sold the house, as I had once run into Alice at a restaurant when I was visiting the Cape a few years back. It was just as I had remembered: a white brick-front ranch with a breezeway and an attached two-story garage. I walked around to the back of the garage and saw that there was a newly built home right next door with mature trees, which were now somewhat blocking the great view of the bay that I had enjoyed so many times from Art's balcony. I continued to walk down his street to the beach, Art's beach. I was shocked to see the huge new home being built right on the waterfront side of the street. I had a hard time figuring out if the small entrance to the beach still existed. I finally found the almost-hidden path and made my way to the beach and the water's edge. I breathed in the salt air, but I didn't stay long as it was getting chilly and the sun was beginning to set. I did take time to walk to the creek. It was high tide, so I couldn't cross over to the jetty. In the twilight, I saw a man with his bike on the other side of the water. I spontaneously shouted over to him," Do you know what this stream is called?"

He thought for a moment and yelled back, "I think it's Snow Creek."

"Thanks," I called back.

I was so happy to now have a name for Art's creek. I checked that off my list of items to find.

The next morning, before I left for a day of exploring, I enjoyed a continental breakfast of tea and a homemade blueberry muffin on the deck. Once again, I preferred to walk. I crossed the street and took my shoes off to walk along the water's edge at Veterans Park. I had only walked a short distance when I passed a couple of men fishing from the shore. I continued my walk until I climbed over the jetty. This time, it was low tide, so I was able to wade across Snow Creek to get to Art's beach. I sat in the sand with my back against a warm rock wall and contemplated the many times I had done that before. I soon heard voices coming down the path and two women arrived at the beach. I didn't hesitate to say hello and they responded with a friendly greeting. *Here's my chance,* I thought to myself. "Hey, do you by any chance know the name of this cute little secret beach?"

The one woman answered immediately with a big smile,

"Secret Beach."

"Really?" I said. "It's called Secret Beach?"

"Yes," she replied. "We've always called it Secret Beach. Even with this huge newly built house going up, as residents of the neighborhood streets, we have a deeded right-of-way to always be able to access this beach."

"It's so great that you will always be able to come here," I replied. "I used to come visit my brother when he lived up the street, and I would often come here and had always wondered if it had a name. Thanks for your help. Enjoy your day."

So far, my research was going well. Next...

I stayed awhile, just watching the seagulls and enjoying my bare feet in the warm sand. I looked back across the jetty at the two fishermen that I had passed. *OK, it's now or never,* I said to myself. I had a photo on my phone of Art and a friend holding up huge fish and I wanted to know what kind of fish they were. Who better to ask than a fisherman? So I crossed back over the creek, walked along the shore, and when I came to one of the fishermen, I said, "Excuse me, can I ask you a fishing question?" He held on to his line and when he turned to look at me, I almost gasped out loud. He looked like Art—baseball hat, full dark beard, and a twinkle in his eye.

"Sure," he said. "How can I help you?"

Gathering my composure the best that I could, I said, "I've got this picture of my brother and his friend each holding up a fish. I was wondering if you could tell me what kind of fish they are?"

"Well, that's easy," he said. "It's a bass."

"Really?" I said. "You can identify it that easily?"

"Sure can," he said. "That's what we're fishing for too. Looks like he won a prize for that one. See that official stamped insignia on the photo? Means he caught a big one."

"Oh my God," I said. "I didn't even notice that. Thanks for pointing it out."

I briefly told him Art's story and how I had spent a lot of time at the Cape with him. I then asked, "Are you from the area? You might have known him."

"No," he answered. "Afraid not. We're from Alaska. We come here in the fall when our fishing season is over in our area. There's some of the best fishing in the world right here at the Cape."

"Well, thanks for your help. I will have to check into this award," I said. "Enjoy your day."

"Oh, happy to help," he said. "And sorry about the loss of your brother."

I turned and walked on down the beach, feeling like I had just had a visit with Art. I smiled to myself. *Maybe Art had sent a look-alike angel to help me? That would so be Art.* I could still hear him saying, "Are you having fun?"

I was feeling good about my research, so I decided it was time to take a drive and continue my adventure.

I set my Google Maps for Barnstable Village, even though I knew that the hospice house had been sold to a place called Latham

Center, which now was a facility that provided residential and independent living opportunities for those with complex special needs. I still just had to visit it. I crossed Main Street in Hyannis and shortly was at the rotary to Route 132. The memories came flooding back to the day Eileen and I took Art to the hospice. It was pouring rain and without Google Maps or a GPS, I didn't know where I was going. I remembered that I had my handwritten directions clutched in my hand...oh my, such a trip. It did not take as long as I had remembered to arrive at Barnstable Village, maybe only twenty minutes. I took a left on Railroad Avenue, and at the end of the dead-end street, there it was. A two-story Colonial that was now partially vinyl-sided on the front and had very worn natural cedar shakes on the sides and back. I parked my car and wondered if I should even try to get into the building. What was I looking for? What did I think I would find? I knocked at the front door. After a couple of tries, a man opened the door just a crack. He looked forty-ish, with disheveled hair and sleepy eyes as though I had just woken him. "What do you want?" he asked. I immediately knew I had made a mistake in coming here.

I assumed he was a resident of the facility, so I said, "I'm sorry, I must have the wrong address." Without responding, he immediately shut the door. As I put my tail between my legs and walked to my car, I felt disappointed, yet I couldn't resist taking a walk around back. Just maybe the brick walk was still there with Art's brick. It was not. There was no brick patio. Feeling defeated, I knew after twenty-four years, I couldn't expect to see the wind-chimes outside of what had been Art's room, but in my heart, I heard the tinkling music. Walking back to my car, I realized I was chasing a memory that was not to be found. I have since learned that the bricks from the Barnstable Hospice were moved to the new McCarthy Care Hospice Center in Sandwich, Massachusetts. A destination for my next trip to the Cape.

Next...

Off to my next mission—the John-Lawrence Funeral Home in Marstons Mills. I didn't really want to go inside, but since I could not remember, I wanted to know how long the ride was from the funeral home to the Mosswood Cemetery. Much to my surprise, it was less than a ten-minute ride between the two locations. As I entered through the ornate gates of the cemetery, I thought for sure that I knew where Art's grave was—on the left across from some woods. I drove along where I thought it might be, but I could not find it. Fortunately, just as I was about to give up, along came a groundskeeper riding in an ATV. He stopped and said, "You look lost. Can I help you?"

"I hope so," I said, close to tears. "I'm trying to find my brother's grave. I thought I knew where it was."

Just as I said that, I remembered I had some paperwork that might help.

"Wait; I think I have something," I said.

I searched my front seat for the special folder I had brought with me for this trip. I rummaged through the papers and there it was...a receipt for Art's headstone. The man looked over my shoulder and said, "Section 7, Lot 175, Grave 3. I know where that is. Over there with the singles. Follow me."

We walked over to an area and both began to look at the names on the headstones. It only took me a couple of minutes to find Art's grave.

"Here it is," I shouted as though I had found a prize. "I found it."

Arthur Dean Westfall

1947–1996

Beloved Son, Brother, Uncle, Friend

"Thanks," I said. "I couldn't have found it without you."

"No problem. This happens almost every day. Glad to help," he said as he tipped his baseball cap and drove away.

I looked up to the beautiful blue sky and said, "Thanks, Art, for another guiding angel."

I stayed long enough to place the shells I had picked up on Art's beach on his headstone; one for each sister and one for each of his nieces and nephews. As I looked around, I noticed an empty wrought-iron hook on a nearby tree. With a smile, I vowed that the next time I came back, I would bring a wind chime for Art and hang it on that tree.

Checking another item off my list, I was ready to head back to my B&B in Hyannis. But before I did, I wanted to make one more stop.

I drove to Pufferbellies. I wasn't sure what to expect, but I was surprised to see the building vacant with everything boarded up. The parking lot had grass growing through the cracks in the asphalt and the sign was faded and in disrepair.

Before I had left for my trip to the Cape, I had a conversation with John Morgan, now the previous owner and Art's former boss. He told me he had initially leased the property to a nightclub, and it had changed the venue completely. It seemed to attract a somewhat rough local crowd, even ending with fights and a shooting or two in the parking lot. Eventually, the club was closed down for public safety reasons. I was so sorry to hear this, as I remembered the many summers Art had worked at Pufferbellies when it was the go-to night spot on the Cape. At that time, it was the summer place that many locals and vacationers looked forward to coming back to year after year. John told me he had recently sold the property to the Hy-Line Cruise Company, which was going to demolish the historic building and make a parking lot for the island ferry commuters and tourists. However, I later found out that the Hy-Line Cruises withdrew their request to raze the 118-year-old building to see if it might be possible for the building to be preserved in a manner to benefit the local community. John said he also had heard there was talk of the building being turned into a bus repair station, taking advantage of the roundhouse setup and the location.

Although it was sad to see how much this property had changed, I was glad I had taken the time to pause and remember when this had been Art's happy place. Not only was this where he worked managing Pufferbellies, but this had been his home away from home where he was loved, respected, and had made many friends.

I left Pufferbellies and found I had just enough time to go back to my B&B to refresh and dress for my evening plans. I had made arrangements to meet Debbie Morgan, Art's dear friend, for dinner.

I had recently contacted Deb Morgan and told her about the book that I was writing about Art and that I was coming to do some research at the Cape. She happily agreed to meet me for dinner. I was nervous yet excited to catch up on the past twenty-four years of The Art Westfall Foundation.

I met Deb at The Black Cat in the Hyannis Harbor area. Shawn, the owner/manager of the restaurant, had reserved a special table for us on the covered porch. Although he did not personally know Art, over the years, the restaurant had been a great supporter of The Art Westfall Foundation. Deb and I settled in, ordered our meals, and the waitress brought over a bottle of wine on the house. I felt like royalty, as it seemed Debbie had invited a few other committee members to join us just because of me, Art's sister, who was in town.

Before we even got started on catching up and all my questions, Deb asked me if I would like to present a check from The Art Westfall Foundation to a recipient: a waitress who was a single mom who worked at The Black Cat. She had just broken her foot and was unable to work. I was thrilled to be asked and my eyes filled with tears. As it turned out, she was not there in person, but I was able to present the check to her manager, Shawn, who promised to get the check to her. He too was touched by the generosity of The Art Westfall Foundation.

I didn't know where to begin with all my questions for Debbie. I first asked her to tell me about The Art Westfall foundation board members and who was now running the Foundation. I was shocked to find out that after twenty-four years, the board was still made up of the same group of Art's longtime friends who had started the foundation: Deb Morgan, LuLu Murray, John Shea, Ed Miles, plus a few new volunteers along the way, including John (Beezer) Bearse, Ben Surro, Heather Wilson, and Tanya Johnson. In addition, there had been many bartenders, waitstaff, and hospitality workers who had lent a helping hand with the fundraising.

Deb told me of the many successful fundraisers over the years: The Bartender's Ball, Miracle on Main Santa Stroll, booze cruises in Hyannis Harbor, golf tournaments, and poker runs. More recently, several restaurants had held their own charity events with the proceeds going to The Art Westfall Foundation.

One of the most current fundraisers had been hosted by a local lawyer, John C. Manoog III, who offered a $10,000 grant to match donations to The Art Westfall Foundation. In his youth, John had been a summer worker on the Cape. He started as a dishwasher, worked his way up to a busboy, and eventually ended up as a bartender and bouncer. So, as he said, "I've been there and just wanted to help." With the support of local radio stations and newspapers, John was able to make his matching grant happen.

Deb was proud to tell me that the foundation had now expanded its help to those in the hospitality industry not only on the Cape mainland, but also on the nearby islands of Nantucket and Martha's Vineyard. She also shared that COVID-19 had hit the restaurant and hospitality industry especially hard on the Cape. During this time, The Art Westfall Foundation had given out hundreds of grocery store gift cards to help feed the hospitality workers and their families.

Just as we were discussing what the foundation had been doing all these years, along came another surprise: LuLu Murray, a long-time committee member and another of Art's dear friends of many years. She joined us at our table and began to add her memories to the conversation. LuLu not only shared about working with Art as a bartender both at Mount Snow, Vermont, and the Cape, she shared stories of helping Art through his illness. She mentioned how several times, she had stayed overnight with Art just to keep him company. One of those nights near the end of Art's life, during the time he had the PICC line in his arm with the PAC pump to infuse pain medication, the supply line ran out of medication and Art was in a lot of pain. LuLu said she was scared and didn't know what to do, so she called the hospice number she found on a business card on Art's kitchen counter. Thankfully, hospice responded and sent someone over to help almost immediately. This story touched my heart and reaffirmed to me how so many friends had been a part of caring for Art in his dying process. We continued to talk, laugh, cry, reminisce, and drink wine. I could have listened to their stories all night. Deb went on to tell us of a time during the spring before Art passed. She and a group of Art's friends rented an RV and took him to Foxwoods Casino in Connecticut for a fun outing. Debbie glowed when she told of the memories they had made and how much fun they all had on that special excursion. Deb and LuLu told me about how they had met Art at North Country Fair in Vermont. They reminisced about their years of skiing and working in Vermont in the winters and then working together at the Cape in the summers. They really were the "Snowbirds of the Northeast."

As the evening went on, I asked if either knew of Art's ex-wife, Heather. Deb knew that she had remarried a few years back and that she had recently passed. She also mentioned that Heather's sons, Art's stepsons—the Meagher boys—had supported several of The Art Westfall Foundation's fundraisers and were not only living nearby, but had established a very successful residential and commercial construction business in nearby Osterville. While I had not known the boys very well, I wondered if I should try to contact them.

It was an emotional evening, and I didn't want it to end. I learned so much about what The Art Westfall Foundation had been providing over the last twenty-four years, and I also learned a few more things about Art's close friendships.

Before we ended our time together, I was so happy that Deb encouraged me to keep writing and she agreed to help me with an epilogue for the book.

I left dinner with my heart full, knowing The Art Westfall Foundation was alive, well, and still in the caring hands of his dear friends.

I had one more day left to do research and explore the area. I knew I wanted to do a little journaling before I decided what I was going to do with my last day. Lucky for me, there was a beach right across the street from my B&B. I walked over to the beach and found a great spot on a sand dune surrounded by sea grass. I hunkered down, and while I was writing and daydreaming, I thought what a lovely place this would be for a photo. Since I'm not crazy about selfies and not really good at them either, I was hoping to find someone to take my picture. The beach was deserted with no one in sight. Fortunately, a few minutes later, a man came walking by with his dog along the water's edge. I waved my arm and called to him, and as he got closer, I asked if he wouldn't mind using my phone to take a picture of me. He did, and as things turned out, I loved the photo of me sitting relaxed, barefoot in the sea grass. This photo is the Author's Photo at the back of my book, which was "taken by a man walking his dog on the beach." I wish I could give him credit but have no idea who he was or how I could possibly ever find him. For now, my thanks!

I remembered that I wanted to do one more thing at the harbor: I wanted to find the Cat Boat with the big cat face on the sail, the one that I had watched so many times with Art from his balcony. So off I went, walking down to the harbor one more time. I wasn't exactly sure where the Cat Boat had docked but I knew it had been somewhere along the pier behind Spanky's. I remembered there had been a printed Cat Boat sign nailed onto a mooring pole. I walked up and down the dock area, looking for that sign, and finally realized it just wasn't there. I asked several boaters near the dock, but no one knew what had become of the Cat Boat. Disappointed and feeling defeated, I walked back to my B&B. I stopped in the foyer to check out the rack of tourist flyers that advertised local attractions, just in case there was something that I might want to do before I left the Cape. And there it was...a glossy brochure with a photo of the Cat Boat! Not just any cat boat, but my Cat Boat. I immediately googled the contact information on my computer. I found out several things: first, a catboat is a style of sailboat, which I did not know. Second, this boat in particular was actually named Eventide, and lastly, after almost three decades of chartering passengers on his catboat, the captain of the ship, Marcus Sherman, had retired in 2017 and just passed away in April 2020. I was grateful for the information, and I will always hold fond memories of "my catboat."

Time was going by quickly on my last day, and I only had the afternoon left before I was to head home. I kept thinking of the Meagher boys, Art's stepsons. I didn't know if they would remember me or be willing to talk with me, but I knew I had to try.

Next stop: Osterville. I found that the little town wasn't very far and easy to find. I parked my car and walked down Main Street, looking in the high-end shops and gathering my courage. Just as I was about to change my mind, I saw it... a nicely lettered sign, Meagher Construction, Inc., hanging over the door of a newer white building with navy-blue shutters, looking very Cape Cod.

I said to myself, *Well, I'm here, so I might as well go in.* I explained to the receptionist who I was and asked if any of the Meagher boys were around. She said they were not, but she would get someone to help me. Shortly, a nice thirty-something young man greeted me. "How can I help you?" he asked.

I found myself stumbling, trying to tell him who I was. "Well, I'm Art Westfall's sister. He was married to the Meagher boy's mother, Heather, and I am writing a book and trying to connect with the boys." It sounded so lame, but I didn't know what else to say.

He politely said, "Oh, that's nice. The boys are out on jobs, but I'll have Tim call you."

I hesitated, wondering if this had been a good idea or if I should just forget about it. I thanked the nice young man and gave him my cell number, not expecting to hear from anyone. I breathed a sigh of relief, left the office, and continued walking along the street, looking at the beautiful window boxes in full bloom. Not ten minutes later, my phone rang—it was Tim Meagher.

"Hi, Tim," I said. "I don't know if you remember me?" I explained I was Art's sister and told him I was writing a book about Art and wondered if I could ask him a few questions.

He hesitantly agreed, but asked, "What kind of questions?"

Before I asked him anything, I offered my condolences on the recent loss of his mom.

Tim then softened and said, "Thank you. She came to live with me and my family before she passed." He continued to say, "I was so glad that I was able to spend time with her in her last months."

He then briefly told me about Meagher Construction. He was the owner and his brothers Matt and Mike worked with him. Since he could hear I was outside trying to have this conversation with street noises in the background, he asked, "How long will you be in the area?"

"I am planning on leaving in the morning, but I would stay if we could meet."

"How about I try and get my brothers together to have breakfast with you tomorrow morning? I don't know if it will work, but I'll get back to you."

"That would be great," I said. "I'll wait to hear from you."

I was excited and nervous about the possibility of getting together with the boys. I did not hear from Tim that night, so I had breakfast in the morning at the B&B and killed some time, hoping that he would call. Finally, I decided that it probably was not going to happen. I packed my bags and headed home. Since a part of me really wasn't ready to leave the Cape, I decided to take the scenic Route 6A on my way home.

I stopped at a very nice yarn store, The Black Purls, where I enjoyed a conversation with the owner, who told me the profits from the store all go to help those in need. She explained that the recipients were required to be employed and had to be trying to help themselves. She said this was a "hand up and not a hand-out." I was so impressed by her generosity and vowed to bring my knitting group back to her shop someday.

As I kept driving, along came another surprise gift. I went right past Maki Monument! This had been one of the last places on my research list. I decided I was right there and might as well do it. I drove a little further down the road until I could turn around and went back. A female employee asked to help me. I once again explained that I was writing a book and what I wanted to know was if in fact there really was a Mr. Maki, as I had called him in my book. She assured me that, yes, there was a Mr. Maki, and he was her father. She reached behind her in a file drawer and pulled out Art's file with a copy of my personal check, which I had written to order Art's headstone.

Twenty-four years later…another piece of the puzzle.

I continued along Route 6A, heading toward the Sagamore Bridge. Just when I felt I was ready to leave the Cape and go home, my cell phone rang. I don't ever answer calls when I am driving, but this time I did. It was Tim Meagher. "Hey," he said. "It's Tim. I'm sorry I didn't get back to you last night. I tried to set something up with my brothers but breakfast just didn't work for them."

"That's OK," I said. "I'm driving; would you mind waiting a minute while I pull over?"

He agreed, and I was so happy to hear from him that I almost forgot the questions I wanted to ask. Once I found a place to pull over, I said, "OK, any chance I could ask you a couple of quick questions?"

"Sure," he said. "I'll try and help you if I can."

"Great," I said. "I'm trying to figure out how old you and your brothers were when Art married your mother, any idea?"

Tim thought for a moment and said, "Well, I am forty-one, Matt is forty-six, and Mike is forty-eight, so doing the math would have made me about six, Matt eleven, and I guess Mike thirteen."

"Yikes," I said. "I can't believe you guys are in your forties!"

"OK, next," I said, so excited to be getting some answers to my questions. "Any chance you know the make of Art's convertible?"

"Oh, that's an easy one. It was a Chrysler LeBaron," he immediately answered. Then he quietly said, "I also remember that when Art could no longer drive, he gave that car to my brother, Matt."

"Gosh, thanks. I didn't know that," I said. "Got time for one more?"

"No problem, go for it," he said.

"Oh my God, this is so helpful," I said, writing as fast as I could. "OK," I said, trying to stay focused and remember the questions that I needed answered. "Tim, do you by any chance know the other man in the photo of Art with the prize bass?"

"I do," he said. "He was a good friend of Art's named Gary Brown." Tim laughed when he shared that Gary had actually caught a bigger bass only a few weeks later and topped Art's prize fish.

Tim then said, "Here's another fishing story for you. I remember a time when I was only eight or nine...I was fishing with

Art offshore in Wellfleet and I caught a six-foot blue shark. I was so scared that I dropped my line and ran." He laughed when he continued, "Art picked up my pole and pulled it in." He then said, "There was even an article in the *Cape Cod Times,* and I still remember the headline: 'Pint-Size Boy Catches Quart-Size Shark.'"

"That was a great story," I said, reminding me of the closeness Tim had with Art. "Thank you so much for sharing it and helping me with my questions."

"Oh, no problem," he said. "Glad I could help. Would you want to get together later today?"

"Thanks for the offer," I said, "but I'm just about to cross the bridge and head back to Connecticut."

"I understand," he said. "But next time you're in town, let's get together so you can meet my wife and three kids."

I thanked him and we said our goodbyes. I was so happy that I had made this connection with Tim, and I left looking forward to meeting him and his brothers in person the next time I visited the Cape.

Now it really was time for me to go home.

After my research trip to the Cape, I found myself in a bit of a writer's funk about the book. I questioned not only whether it was good enough, but I was also aware that I was writing it only from a sister's perspective, and I still really didn't know a lot about the rest of Art's life.

I knew little of Art's years of skiing in Vermont and not much about the years he had gone back and forth to the Cape in the summers. I didn't know about his friends or the lifestyle they had created. I knew even less about his marriage to Heather and their years together with her boys.

What was I going to do? Continue to write the best that I could or maybe forget the whole book?

Fortunately, my writing mentor, "C", convinced me to keep going and that yes, the book was from a sister's perspective, and yes, it was enough.

But it wasn't enough for me. I decided to try to contact some of Art's friends. After interviewing several people from different parts of Art's life—a high school friend, a fellow skier, and his former boss—their stories of Art not only warmed my heart, but served to confirm that I didn't need to look further. What I knew about Art already as a brother was true across the board. He was a beloved, really special guy...

Arthur Dean Westfall

1947–1996

Son, Brother, Uncle, Friend

Satisfied that I had done my best, I could hear Art saying, "Are you having fun?" I searched on YouTube until I found his favorite song, "Little Darlin'" by The Diamonds, and...I danced.

EPILOGUE

The overstuffed manila envelope could not be closed, as it contained tales of hardship, thank-you notes, cards, and letters, all in appreciation from over twenty-eight years of The Art Westfall Foundation. The foundation was formed out of recognition of a great giver, Art Westfall. The foundation that bears his name can't be measured by the number of recipients or the amount of money raised and distributed, but in those letters of all who have benefited from the generosity of fellow Cape residents and islanders.

Everything contained in the envelope, along with hundreds of messages on our website, spoke to one's loss, illness, or accident, times of struggle to make ends meet during trying times in their lives. Over two hundred and seventeen recipients of financial support from AWF helped make a difference. Many without insurance and depleted funds were faced with rent or mortgage payments, an unexpected car repair, or food for their family. AWF stepped in and helped where we could.

Each story uniquely stands on its own:

The single mom who was supporting her son by working as a waitress. Upon coming home from work one evening, she let her dog out in the backyard, broke her ankle in a lawn divot, and in the process of bracing her fall, broke her other ankle. She would not be able to work for months. The restaurant did not offer medical insurance or even sick days. The AWF stepped in.

The restaurant in Hyannis that caught fire one evening. The next day, twenty-three people had lost their jobs and would not receive unemployment for a few weeks. The AWF helped bridge the gap.

A Brazilian father, swimming with his two sons, drowned one beautiful day in an Osterville pond. The community was devastated. The AWF funded the funeral expenses for the family.

Two hundred and seventeen unique stories with everything from assisting with the expense of funerals to hundreds of grocery store gift cards, plus financial assistance with medical payments and, on some very sad occasions, money for the family to make their wish to spend precious time with loved ones come true.

Even when AWF struggled with our own financing due to a freak weather event, hurting the attendance of a fundraiser, or our own inability to raise money during the pandemic, we persevered by the generosity of some incredible people. A local attorney and past hospitality worker donated a large sum of money that allowed us to continue. The AWF was down, but never out.

In need of new ideas and direction, Heather Wilson and Tanya Johnson volunteered to lead us for the next few years. They turned a birthday celebration into "The Miracle on Main," raising thousands of dollars while giving all of us a fun day and a chance to celebrate with each other.

We must also give thanks to so many business owners for their donation of time, staff, food, and facilities, helping to assist in the making of our moniker "Friends Helping Friends."

We started AWF in 1995 to help our friend Artie, whose suggestion led to the organization being formed. Today, the AWF continues to assist our friends in the hospitality community on the Cape and the islands.

Lastly, I could not have done it without the dedication, hard work, and loving friendship of the board members listed below. They were all there from the start, and I hope they continue into the future.

"Friends Helping Friends"
Deb Morgan

Board of Directors:
John (Beazer) Bearse
Edward Miles
Debora (Deb) Morgan
Louise (LuLu) Murray
John Shea
Ben Surro

ACKNOWLEDGMENTS

Where do I begin to thank the many people who have supported me in the writing of this book? The beginning...my heartfelt thanks to "C", Carole Flanagan Flynn, for her belief in me, for her encouragement, and for her expertise in editing. You are dearly missed by so many.

Thank you to my readers: Deb Morgan, Shelia Powers, and my daughter Jennifer Pulisic. Your edits, suggestions, and support meant so much.

A special thanks to my sister Eileen, who not only lived this story with me, but was always "there" for the many times I called her and said, "gotta a minute—can I read something to you?"

Thank you to the writers in my classes who nudged me along and especially to my dear friend Mary, who not only took my first writing class with me, but continued to read and reread as I edited each chapter.

Appreciation to Randy Ritter and Jeff MacDonald for their computer support.

Thanks to my granddaughter, Allie Pulisic, for her graphic expertise in designing the Coming Soon card.

A huge thank you to my friend Chris, who saved me when I lost my edited manuscript somewhere in cyberspace and helped me retrieve it!

A big thank you to Jenny and Megan at Elite Authors for your patience in answering all my questions and your quick responses to my SOS emails! And, to the Elite Project team including the proof readers and cover designer who took this journey with me and helped to make this book happen.

Thank you to the AWF board members, especially Deb Morgan, who was my cheerleader, and to Art's friends who were willing to share their stories about Art: Ed Miles, LuLu Murray, John Morgan, Jack and Peggy Chernock,and Tim Meagher. My special thanks to Kelly, who let me include her personal letter to the Westfall sisters.

Thank you to my sisters, Charlotte Westfall Ritter and Eileen Westfall Acampora, for your help in remembering some of our childhood events and your ever-loving support…even allowing me to read the book to you four days in a row on our favorite beach in Milford, Connecticut.

And to my parents, thank you for your courage to leave the coal mining town in West Virginia and move to Connecticut.

The Art Westfall Foundation
"Friends Helping Friends"

A nonprofit organization that provides emergency financial assistance to those in need in the hospitality industry of the Cape and the nearby islands of Nantucket and Martha's Vineyard.

Please join us in our efforts by contributing to The Art Westfall Foundation. Your donations will help keep our mission going!

The Art Westfall Foundation
330 Willow Street
West Barnstable, MA 02668
artwestfallfoundation@gmail.com

All proceeds from the sale of this book will go to
The Art Westfall Foundation.

Art and the Westfall sisters